The Last Station

The Last Station

Naguib Mahfouz Looking Back

Mohamed Salmawy

Translated by
Andy Smart and Nadia Fouda-Smart

The American University in Cairo Press
Cairo New York

Translations of Dreams quoted in this edition are from *The Dreams* (AUC Press, 2004) and *Dreams of Departure* (AUC Press, 2007), except those on pages 6, 64, 71, 72, 79, and 112–13.

First published in 2007 by
The American University in Cairo Press
113 Sharia Kasr El Aini, Cairo, Egypt
420 Fifth Avenue, New York, NY 10018
www.aucpress.com

Dar el Kutub No. 13903/07
ISBN 978 977 416 125 4

Dar el Kutub Cataloging-in-Publication Data

Salmawy, Mohamed
The Last Station: Naguib Mahfouz Looking Back / Mohamed Salmawy; translated by Andy Smart and Nadia Fouda-Smart.—Cairo: The American University in Cairo Press, 2007
p. cm.
ISBN 977 416 125 4
I. Andy, Smart (trans.) II. Fouda-Smart, Nadia (jt. trans.)
III. Title
928.1

1 2 3 4 5 6 7 8 9 10 12 11 10 09 08 07

Designed by Andrea El-Akshar/AUC Press Design Center
Printed in Egypt

To Umm Kulthum and Fatma Naguib Mahfouz,
who were the first to read the draft of this book

M.S.

Preface

To relive a painful experience is even more painful than the experience itself. The first time around one is caught unawares while the second time one recollects it deliberately, moment by moment, event by event, and the reaction is greater.

That is the story of this book, in whose pages I have tried to recapture the experience of the final forty-five days of the life of the late novelist Naguib Mahfouz, from the moment he entered the hospital on Sunday 16 July 2006 until he was laid to rest on Thursday 31 August, that same year, including all the painful feelings that awaited us as well as the moments of joy that the patient in room 612 gave to his visitors.

Although I have generally recorded the facts of what happened without interpretation or analysis I know there are people who would prefer some of the events of this time to remain undisclosed. However, this was an experience that I was destined to witness and I could not withhold my testimony.

This book is not simply a record of the period that the Ustaz spent in the hospital before his death. It is more an attempt, through diary form, to offer an impression of a man who had no equal, whether in regard to his personal integrity, his unique personality, or his unprecedented literary achievement. It tries to present an honest view of a man through a relationship that continued from the time we first met in the seventies until I carried his bier on my shoulder more than three decades later.

Is it a definitive testimony?

I cannot say, for such a testimony needs more than a single book. But at least with these pages I have laid a foundation stone in an attempt to record the details of the final stage in the life of the Arab world's greatest novelist, Naguib Mahfouz.

One

It was on the morning of Sunday 16 July 2006 that Hagg Muhammad Sabri called me at home anxiously. "What's happened to the Ustaz?" he asked. "I went to read him the newspapers like I do every morning but his guards told me he'd been taken to the hospital and there was no one at home."

I calmed his fears, assuring him that the Ustaz was fine and that I was on my way to see him in the hospital.

The previous evening at six o'clock I'd gone for my regular meeting at the great man's home as I always did on Saturdays—for our weekly interview for the *al-Ahram* newspaper—and as usual we'd sat and talked about various topics.

On this occasion the conversation revolved around the situation in Lebanon, where the Israeli aggression had completely destroyed the south of the country and forced its inhabitants to flee. The number of victims measured hundreds of men, women, and children.

The Ustaz was very distressed about what had happened: "God help us!" he said, "This is awful. How could such destruction become an end in itself?"

His mood wasn't good. His mind was distracted most of the time and his words were heavy with sadness and grief.

We were only half an hour into our conversation. The evening still lay before us and I didn't want to spend the whole time talking about the tragedy in Lebanon.

His wife, Madame Atiyatallah, placed a tray of chocolates in front of me. "What's this?" asked the Ustaz. His sight was not much help to him in those final days.

"Chocolate," I said and added, in jest, "Will you have one?" For the first time he smiled—the last time he'd had chocolate was about forty-five years ago, when his doctors told him to give up sweets after he'd begun suffering from diabetes. For almost half a century he'd followed his doctors' orders and never touched sweets. Naguib Mahfouz was an ideal patient who obeyed doctors' orders to the letter—this was part of the discipline of his character and his love of system and order.

"The kids," he said, meaning his daughters Umm Kulthum and Fatma, "once brought me diabetic chocolate but I didn't eat much of it. Even before I became diabetic I didn't care much for chocolate."

He related how he'd first discovered by pure chance that he had diabetes: "When I reached fifty I went to take out some life insurance. After I'd filled in the form they made me do some medical tests that went on for a whole day and at the end of it all they reprimanded me: 'Why didn't you mention that you have diabetes when you filled the form in?' Until that moment I didn't know I had it. I thought diabetes was caused by some great shock. In fact, I was so shocked by what they'd said that I told them, 'If I didn't already have diabetes you'd have set it off!'"

I asked him, "Doesn't the illness bother you?"

"No, not at all. I'm not the complaining type—you just have to obey the doctor and follow the instructions and it's no bother. Some of my friends don't believe I have diabetes because I lead a very normal life. I do what the doctor says—even the diet they advised me to follow is a way of life, and after a while I forgot I had an illness."

Our conversation turned to the reprinting of his *Dreams in the Time of Convalescence* (published in English as *The Dreams* and *Dreams of Departure*) that Dar El Shorouk was preparing for publication, including some new Dreams published after the first edition had sold out. The number of Dreams had now reached two hundred.

I told him it was at the press. I had enquired about it the day before and been told that the first copy might be ready by the following week. He asked, "Did you give them the six Dreams you had from me last year, to be published in the weekend edition of *al-Ahram*?" I said yes, and that the new edition included all the Dreams published up till now. He was quiet for a moment. "What about the French edition?" he asked. I told him it would be on the market in France the following December, to coincide with his birthday in the first half of the month and Christmas in the second half.

During our conversation about *Dreams in the Time of Convalescence* I felt that Ustaz Naguib had returned from a distant place where he'd been lost to me and was now no longer as distracted as he had been at the beginning of our session. When I got up to say goodbye at the end of the meeting his features had relaxed. "Stay a bit," he said. "We haven't finished chatting and you haven't touched the chocolate!" Then he asked his wife, whom he always addressed formally in front of people, "Madame, why don't you bring him something to drink."

In normal circumstances I'd have demurred and said, "Never mind. I'll be back next Saturday." And he'd have said, "Don't be late," and I would have left. On this day I felt that his mood merited that we should continue our chat a little longer so I agreed to his request and went back to my seat.

As soon as I'd sat down again he said, "I had a dream yesterday!"

"What was it about?" I asked. While he told it to me I recorded it on the tape recorder I'd brought with me.

The Ustaz used to memorize every dream by heart, just the way he wanted it written down. On Tuesdays he'd dictate those dreams to Hagg Sabri who would write them down and read them out to the Ustaz, who would approve them and then put them in a large envelope in the drawer of his desk. In the first week of every month he would send three of them to the magazine *Nisf al-dunya* for publication.

The number of recordings of the Dreams that I collected had grown over the past few years and I often used to go back to the tape recorder to listen to them in his voice. But I didn't know that this would be the last Dream and that this would be the last of the visits I'd been making every Saturday evening to his home at 172 al-Nil Street in Agouza for almost twelve years since the heinous attempt on his life on 14 October 1994. That incident had left his right hand injured—his writing hand—with a partial disability that prevented him from writing, after which his column in *al-Ahram*, at his own request, became a weekly conversation between the two of us, published in the same place that his column used to appear.

I asked him at that time the reason he'd chosen me to do this and he'd replied, "Because you're different from me. I'm a child of the 1919 revolution and you belong to the generation of the 1952 revolution. I'm a novelist, while you're a dramatist. I made my name through realism, while you tend toward absurdist theater. So our conversation will be rich. I don't want someone who agrees with me on everything and who says 'amen' to all I say!"

My relationship with the Ustaz—which went back over thirty years—was never so strong as during these past twelve years, during which time I'd look forward, week after week, to our Saturday session just as much as he did. I knew that through our weekly conversation he felt that his relationship with his readers remained unbroken. Every time a letter arrived at the newspaper from one of his readers, about something he'd written, I was careful to read it out to him, however simple or insignificant its content, in order to preserve this relationship that I felt he valued so much. I often used to pay the price for this, since he always had to reply to every letter that reached him. In recent years he'd entrusted me with this task and I couldn't turn up the following week without him asking me, "Did you send the letter to the reader who asked for a copy of the novel *The Beginning and the End*?" Or, "Did you write to that young man who sent us his short story?"

I discovered that for many years he'd been answering these letters himself, by hand. A number of originals of these letters later reached me, which their owners had kept for many years before deciding to donate them to me. I don't know how this great novelist found time to reply to all those letters, in spite of a daily program that took up every available minute and which he followed for years without modification.

In that last meeting I read to him one of these letters in which a reader was admiring what he'd said in a previous interview. "Leave this one with me," he said. "I'll ask Hagg Sabri to answer it. It only needs a word of thanks and I don't want to trouble you with it."

So this was to be our last Saturday. Our weekly sessions would come to an end in the evening of 15 July 2006. The Ustaz would not receive me the next Saturday or any other Saturday in the reception room of his home, wearing his dressing gown—silk in summer and wool in winter—and his leather slippers, putting on his glasses and the hearing aid in his left ear, and saying to me with open arms, "*Ahlan, ahlan,*" before kissing me on both shoulders, because he never kissed anyone on the face.

For the next day, in the early hours of the morning, he tripped over in his bedroom and fell to the floor, injuring himself on the back of his head. His younger daughter Fatma came in to find him unconscious and bleeding badly. His personal guard helped her to get him immediately to the Police Hospital, beside his home, where he received a few stitches in the head and from where he was supposed to be discharged within a few days.

As soon as he had regained consciousness after the operation he found me there in front of him. "What happened?" he asked. I explained that he'd tripped over, as we all do, that he'd been taken to the hospital for a couple of stitches and that he'd be out in a few days.

His wife, Madame Atiyatallah, was sitting with him in the room while Hala, the nurse, stood beside his bed. The Ustaz immediately recognised the nurse as the one who'd looked after him when he'd entered the same hospital in the winter of 1994, following the attempted assassination. He greeted her and asked us, "Are we in the Police Hospital?"

"Yes," I replied."

"A couple of stitches, you say?"

"Yes."

He laughed and said, "So I've been stitched up by the police now!"

We all laughed with him but his own laugh resounded more loudly.

I spent some time with the doctors to reassure myself about his condition. They'd performed a scan on his head to check whether there was any effect from the fall and found everything normal. They told me they would do another scan after twenty-four hours, since some effects on the brain would appear only after a while.

He was in good spirits, better than the previous evening when he'd been preoccupied by the war in Lebanon. So when he asked me on this visit about the situation in Lebanon I didn't want to distress him and said, "I haven't seen the news yet—I came as soon as I woke up."

I stayed with him for half an hour. He asked if I'd read the new Dreams that had been published in that day's edition of *Nisf al-dunya* magazine.

"I've seen them," I replied.

"Which dream did you like the most?"

"The last one."

"Which one is that?"

I had the magazine with me, so I read it out:

> I saw myself preparing the table, where the voices of the guests in the next room reached me—the voices of my mother, brothers, and sisters—and while I was waiting I fell asleep. Then I awoke, impatient, and rushed into the next room to invite them in. I found the room completely empty, totally silent, and for a minute I was frightened before I gradually remembered that they'd all passed away and that I'd attended their funerals, one after the other.

An involuntary shiver passed through my body and I wished I'd never set eyes on such a dream.

Two

On his first day in the hospital he was calm. I went back to see him in the afternoon and found him awake. His wife, who stayed in the room from morning till night, was with him. His two daughters, Umm Kulthum and Fatma—or Hoda and Faten, as they were called at home—were also there, as well as several nurses around his bed. There was a playful atmosphere in the room thanks to the high spirits of our model patient who did just as the doctors told him, pleasantly and without grumbling. His presence spread joy throughout room 612. The only thing that showed he was ill was the dressing around his head and a blood bag hanging beside the bed, replacing the blood that he'd lost.

His face lit up when he saw me. "Welcome, dear friend," he said.

"Have you had your lunch, Ustaz Naguib?" I asked.

He replied immediately, "Well, was I going to wait till now?"

"What did you have?"

"Fish." Fish was one of his favorites.

All the indications pointed to him leaving the hospital within a few days—everything seemed to be going well. I asked about the new MRI scan and they told me it was due the next morning. Before going up to the room I'd stopped by to see the hospital manager, General Emad,

He'd assured me that all the results were positive, that they were only keeping the Ustaz in the hospital to rest and that he would soon resume his normal life.

I decided not to tell the press about the Ustaz's situation, to avoid turning the hospital into a paparazzi circus. The most important thing was that he should rest for an extra day without being disturbed by people inquiring after his health. Who knows, maybe he'd be back home before anyone knew he'd even been in the hospital. Under normal circumstances, after a simple suture he'd have been discharged the same day and gone back the following week to have the stitches removed. The doctors had confirmed that when the Ustaz left the hospital they would come to his home to remove the stitches, so that he would not need to return to the hospital.

But by the next day—Monday 17 July 2006—the news had already spread amongst his friends, who'd missed him on Sunday at the Shepheard Hotel, as well as those who would not be meeting him that evening at the Mövenpick. Some of them were starting to wonder what had happened and why the Ustaz hadn't come. I knew then that the time had come to announce the news so I wrote the news story myself, in words that wouldn't cause alarm, for the following day's edition of *al-Ahram*.

The first to check up on him after the news was published was President Mubarak, whose office called the Ustaz's wife, Madame Atiyatallah. The spokesman told her that the president wished to speak to the Ustaz. Madame Atiyatallah thanked the spokesman and told him that the Ustaz did not speak on the phone since he was hard of hearing. The spokesman excused himself for a few moments and then came back to say that the president wished to send his greetings to the Ustaz and had asked if she needed anything, so she requested him to convey thanks to the president from her and her family.

The same day the prime minister, Ahmad Nazif, and the ministers of the interior and of information all called to check on the Ustaz. The minister of culture, Farouk Hosni, then came by, followed by dignitaries, friends and acquaintances, and men of letters including Gamal al-Ghitani, Yusif al-Qa'id, Abd al-Rahman al-Abnoudi, Tawfiq Salih, Naim Sabri, Mamduh al-Laithi, Dr. Fathi Hashim, and many others.

When Ibrahim al-Mu‘allim, his publisher, arrived, the Ustaz greeted him: "Welcome to a dear one, son of a dear one!" al-Mu‘allim placed a chair beside the bed and spent half an hour telling the Ustaz the details of a project I'd put to him before he'd arrived at the hospital. This was the celebration that the Writers Union was planning to hold, with Dar El Shorouk, at the end of the year when the Ustaz would turn ninety-five. Arab and foreign academics and translators would be invited to a conference on Naguib Mahfouz and his work, as well as on issues to do with translating his work abroad. We were aware that up till now 460 translations had been published internationally in over thirty languages, while Dar El Shorouk was about to publish for the first time a deluxe edition of his complete works in Arabic.

The Ustaz listened with interest to all the details. I knew that he preferred this kind of celebration to the ones he found himself forced into every year, when people would bring a birthday cake and he'd have to blow out the candles in front of the cameras. He had never got used to birthday parties, even as a child. He often said to me, "I didn't use to blow candles out when I was a boy so how come I have to blow them out now that I'm a wise old sheikh?!" The first birthday party that he'd had was his fiftieth, given in 1961 by Muhammad Hassanein Heikal. Heikal had invited the legendary diva of Arabic song, Umm Kulthum, after finding out that Mahfouz admired her hugely but had never met her. There were also a number of writers at this party, including Tawfiq al-Hakim and Salah Jahin.

I remember before his ninetieth birthday that I'd called for this particular celebration to be of a standard fitting for one of the country's greatest icons: "As he completes his ninetieth year," I wrote, "why not erect a statue of him in a public square or name a main street after him. This would be our gift to a man who has enriched our lives and raised our standing among nations."

In fact, upon the publication of this article I received a call from the governor of Giza at that time—Mahmud Abul Layl, subsequently the minister of justice—in which he expressed a great interest in this project and said that he had a present for Naguib Mahfouz. The governor kept his promise and asked a professor at the Faculty of Fine Arts to do a mural in mosaic, representing Naguib Mahfouz amidst his works. The mural was placed beneath the 6 October Bridge, facing the writer's home on the corniche in Agouza. The governor also decided to dedicate Sphinx Square, the largest square in Giza, at the beginning of Gam'at al-Duwal Street, to Naguib Mahfouz, thereby renaming it Naguib Mahfouz Square. At the same time the sculptor Sayed Abdu Selim was commissioned to do a life-size bronze statue of the Ustaz with his famous walking stick. The statue was placed in the center of the square. Other than that, birthday presents for Mahfouz were a long succession of birthday cakes, brought by people who would have their picture taken with him as he blew out the candles.

As soon as Ibrahim al-Mu'allim had left, the hospital began to swarm with members of the public coming to check on the great writer of Egypt who they'd read that morning had entered the Police Hospital.

The crowds of visitors continued the next day too and began to be a burden to the Ustaz. The hospital decided to regulate visits strictly and only allow close friends in.

However, preventing visits to the Ustaz was hard on his wife who now had to receive in the waiting room next door all those who couldn't get in to see the Ustaz. Whenever I arrived, or before leaving, I used to pop into that waiting room to greet Madame Atiyatallah or her daughters and I never found an empty seat.

In spite of that, Madame Atiyatallah saw no need to quicken his departure from the hospital. She preferred that he should stay in until he'd had his stitches removed. In the hospital he could receive specialized care that was not available at home, while the barrier that had been erected around him was not possible at home if someone wanted to visit.

On Thursday morning I went to visit him and noticed that he was improving daily. We sat talking about "the state of the nation," as he liked to call it. He told me he'd heard about some demonstrations.

I said, "Yes, in the university, because of Lebanon."

He asked, "Haven't they agreed to a ceasefire yet?"

"Not yet," I said, "but there are some encouraging signs that they soon will." I tried to change the subject so that he wouldn't become upset in the way I'd seen whenever we talked about Lebanon.

"Gabriel García Márquez called in the middle of the night," I said, "apologizing for the time difference, in order to ask after your health."

"Where was he calling from?" he asked.

"From his home in Los Angeles. Throughout the year he moves back and forth between his home in Colombia, his second home in the United States, and his third in Mexico."

We continued talking for some time about Marquéz, whom Mahfouz had never met but with whom he was united by circumstances, such as petitions on issues of freedom that they'd both signed with a number of other international writers. Both of them followed the news of the other from afar and respected the other greatly.

"They say he's not writing any more," Mahfouz commented.

"He's taking a break," I said, "maybe like you did in the early fifties."

"That was at the beginning of my life," said Mahfouz, "but in Marquéz's case it looks like the Nobel curse!"

I was about to ask him what he meant when suddenly the nurse Hala entered, greeting him and commending his progress since the day before. She took his hand in hers and I started to tease him about their special relationship. He always recognized her as soon as she entered the room, whereas whenever anyone else entered the room we had to tell him who it was.

The Ustaz laughed and said, "So? Every time I have an accident she's the one who saves me."

Madame Atiyatallah offered me a cold drink from the mini-bar in the room. When I declined, the Ustaz insisted, adding that no one was going to charge me for it! We both laughed, then he said, "You know, the first time I went to meet Tawfiq Bey (by which he meant Tawfiq al-Hakim) he'd asked a mutual friend—the late Muhammad Mitwalli, the head of the Opera House at that time—to introduce us. Mitwalli fixed a time for us and I went to meet him in one of the downtown cafés. As soon as I'd sat at his table the waiter came and asked me what we wanted. I ordered a coffee and he ordered the same, and then suddenly al-Hakim, who was known to be careful with money, said, 'Look, you're going to say, "I'll pay for this" and I'm going to say, "I'll get it." Let each of us each pay for his own, so we don't end up arguing!'

About an hour later it was time for his lunch so I excused myself and asked him if he wanted anything, telling him I would come back the next day.

"Aren't you going to the North Coast?" he asked.

"Not this week," I replied. In summer I used to go with my family every Thursday to spend the weekend on the North Coast but this week I planned to postpone it.

"I'll go next week," I said, "when you're out of the hospital."

Three

When I entered the room I found him surrounded by doctors. "*Ahlan,* boss!" he said.

One of the doctors looked at me in surprise so I told him that the Ustaz had always liked to tease me since my election as head of the Writers Union. Even though I'd recommended at the first opportunity that the board of the union elect Naguib Mahfouz as honorary head, he still teased me now and then.

"You're everyone's boss!" I replied.

After the doctors had left I moved my chair near his bed to tell him some news from the morning papers, since Hagg Sabri no longer came to him as he used to when the Ustaz was at home. As I talked he commented on some of the news items, while on others he did not.

After a short time I asked, "How are the Dreams coming along?" I knew that the Dreams, which had kept him busy these past years, were his favorite topic. At the mention of them his eyes would light up and he'd become enthusiastic, so I would often ask him about them. Whenever a new collection had been published at the beginning of the month we'd discuss them at length. In spite of his literary skills and his capacity to dazzle us all with whatever he put his hand to, Mahfouz always wanted to know what people thought about what he'd written, as if he were just a beginner who needed other people's approval!

A visiting Spanish critic once asked him in my presence if the innovative form of writing in the dreams was inspired by an ancient Arab tradition. He replied very simply, "No." I complemented his rather brief and modest reply by saying that this form was his own creation and that it was just as new to us as it was in Western literature.

In fact, if we examine the extremely short format that Naguib Mahfouz chose as a vehicle for the Dreams we find that what it most resembles among world literature is Japanese haiku poetry, in which a verse is never more than two or three lines long but which carries more meaning than could be expressed in several pages. He was, however, not influenced by haiku. I once asked him if he'd ever read any haiku; he said he'd heard of it but had never read any.

The Dreams were not separate from Mahfouz's literary output; they were a natural extension of the artistic form that he'd employed, for example, in his *Echoes of an Autobiography*. Although in the *Autobiography* a fine thread joined a series of little pearls, in the Dreams each pearl was self-contained. We have to search for the artistic meaning of each Dream inside itself and not in relation to what comes before or after. As for their content, the Dreams encompassed a sublime and noble vision that comes to an artist only in later life, after he has experienced the full range of life and arrived at a complete wisdom that leads to an inner peace not found earlier on. These are the feelings induced for example by the quartets that Beethoven wrote toward the end of his life, after he'd left behind the sound of a 120-strong philharmonic orchestra, as in the choral Ninth Symphony, and had chosen just four stringed instruments to perform his composition; with these he was able to express a rare spiritual perspective that the complete orchestra was perhaps incapable of doing.

Mahfouz's modesty was such that when someone asked him what he was writing, after he'd begun work on the Dreams, he'd reply by holding out his hand and saying, "Little things, the size of my palm!"

I would then remember the Arabic child's riddle, "What's the size of your palm, and can kill a thousand?" (the answer of course being, "a head-lice comb").

I often remembered this modesty of the Ustaz whenever he had an important visitor who came to pay their respects. Each time a new collection of Dreams was published and he asked me for my opinion, I'd recall some of those writers, who were considered to be among the greatest in the world and who'd made an effort to visit him in order to express their admiration. There was Nadine Gordimer, the South African Nobel laureate, to whom I extended an invitation from Farouk Hosni, the minister of culture, to visit Egypt. She told me she'd visited Egypt many times already but had never managed to meet Naguib Mahfouz. She made it a condition that she would accept the invitation if a meeting could be arranged with the great Egyptian writer.

I remembered the French writer Robert Solé who told him, "You are the world's greatest living storyteller. You have influenced not only readers, but writers too."

I remembered the American poet Laban Carrick Hill, who told Mahfouz how his novel *The Road*—which Mahfouz wrote in 1964 and which was translated into English in 1987, that is, before he won the Nobel prize—had changed the course of his life. I remembered also how the director of the French publishing house Le Rocher had read the French version of some of the Dreams that we'd published in *al-Ahram Hebdo* and said that he'd never read anything like it. He had requested the rights to publish it in France even though at that time the Dreams had not yet been published in book form in Arabic. It was published in Arabic in Egypt only in the year following its French publication. Such urgency to publish the work of an Arab writer abroad, even before publication in his own country, had never been seen before in the Arab world.

All of that was on my mind when I asked the Ustaz in the hospital, "What news of the Dreams?"

He smiled and said, "The Dreams are injured!" I said the doctors had told me that they would remove the stitches that day and he said, "Maybe the Dreams will return after that!"

I added that Amr Mousa, the secretary general of the Arab League, had called me from Lebanon to ask about him and had said that he would come and visit him as soon as he got back. The previous day I'd seen the wife of the British ambassador, Sir Derek Plumbly—who was also the daughter of the late Egyptian novelist Yusif Gohar. She had wanted to pay a visit with her husband for some time, but I'd had to tell her that visits were not allowed at the moment.

The Ustaz said, "Tell her I'd be happy to meet her and the ambassador at home when I get out, God willing."

I had with me a letter for him that I now took out. "This is an invitation from Spain," I said, "to attend a meeting of Nobel prize-winners that's taking place in Madrid. I've sent them your regrets." Then I added, "Did you know, Ustaz Naguib, that Spanish is the language that your work has been translated into most?"

"More than English or French?"

"Yes," I replied. "They've done thirty-nine of your books in Spanish up till now. After that comes English with thirty-one, then French with thirty."

"Anyway," he said, "my thanks to all of them."

"You are the Nobel winner whose work receives a better and better response each year," I said and then added, "Last summer, while I was in Paris, I looked for something by Claude Simon but I didn't find anything in the bookshops, even though he won the Nobel prize before you did."

"Yes," he said, "he won it in 1985 and I was happy to meet him when he came to Cairo."

"I remember it well," I said. "He's a great writer but nowadays you can hardly find his books in the shops, whereas I always find a new book of yours whenever I travel abroad."

It was time for me to leave but his wife asked if I could stay for a while. She'd been told that the minister of health, Dr. Hatem al-Gabali, was coming to visit shortly in order to examine Mahfouz for himself and see how he was doing. I told her I'd call to find out the result of the check-up. I kissed the Ustaz's head and left. (When I called later she said the minister had spent a long time doing the check-up and had expressed his view that there was no need for the Ustaz to go abroad. Since his family hadn't suggested that he should go abroad we imagined that maybe the state had wanted to find out for itself whether his condition called for it!)

While I was on my way out of the hospital, my secretary called me to say she wasn't able to handle the calls that were coming in from all over the world to ask about the health of the Ustaz. She said she'd taken calls from Paris, New York, Morocco, Tunisia, Libya, Spain, Italy, Russia, India, and Korea.

"Hold on, hold on," I said, "I'm on my way."

Before I left, I stopped at the hospital manager's office who reassured me that everything was fine and that the Ustaz could leave at any time he wished.

"Since the stitches will be taken out today he doesn't need to stay any longer," I said.

He agreed. "We'd like the decision to discharge him to be his own and not the hospital's. We're happy to have him here as long as he or his family feels it's better for him to stay."

"That's what he'll want," I continued. "He doesn't like to be away from his friends too much. He likes to stick to his daily routines, which is important psychologically at his age."

Four

I reached the hospital early in the morning, and if I hadn't known that the Ustaz usually woke up early I would have gone on to my office and come back later. Naguib Mahfouz always used to wake up around five or five thirty because in his younger days he would leave his home in Agouza by six, heading south along the Nile as far as Galaa Bridge, and then east across the Gazira Island, past the new Opera House, to Qasr al-Nil Bridge. He would cross the bridge to the Ali Baba cafeteria on Tahrir Square, where he'd go up to the first floor. He'd sit next to the window overlooking the square and read the papers over his morning coffee. Mahfouz chose this cafeteria because it was one of the few that were open at that time of morning, since it was open twenty-four hours a day.

The Ustaz was not addicted to anything. Even the coffee that he used to like to start his day with, he'd take only a sip or two before placing the saucer on top of the cup and not touch it again. Or rather, you could say he was addicted to order—once he got accustomed to something he would always do it the same way, without variation.

From the cafeteria the Ustaz would make his way over to the American University in Cairo, whose doors opened at nine o'clock. There he would head to the AUC Press, which kept a copy of everything that was published about his books in the foreign press. He would look through them and then walk to his office in *al-Ahram* newspaper.

In fact Mahfouz did not have his own office in *al-Ahram*. He used to share an office on the sixth floor with Dr. Hussein Fawzi and Dr. Bint al-Shati'. When the Ustaz won the Nobel prize it was about a year after Tawfiq al-Hakim had passed away, so *al-Ahram* gave him al-Hakim's office that had remained closed since his death. But Mahfouz always sat on the sofa in the office, the one he'd sat on when he'd visited al-Hakim. Not once did he sit at Tawfiq al-Hakim's former desk.

Ibrahim al-Mu'allim once related to me that an Arab journalist had asked al-Mu'allim to accompany him to a meeting with Naguib Mahfouz, who'd given him an appointment early the next day at the Ali Baba cafeteria. It was the same day that al-Mu'allim was due to meet the eminent lawyer and former minister, Dr. Ahmad Kamal Abul Magd, to ask for his daughter's hand in marriage. Al-Mu'allim attended the meeting with Mahfouz first and then, intoxicated by the ideas he'd heard, went to see Dr. Abul Magd, self-assured and turning over in his mind things that he'd heard from the great writer. Al-Mu'allim made such a good impression on that great intellectual that Dr. Abul Magd agreed to him marrying his daughter!

I reached the Ustaz's room in the hospital before nine in the morning and found him awake, as I'd expected. None of his family had arrived yet but I wasn't the first visitor. I found there a man in his eighties whom the Ustaz introduced me to, saying that he was an old acquaintance from the family of al-Aqqad.

The man greeted me in a dignified manner and left. The Ustaz then told me that he was an adviser in the law courts. I asked him if he was related to al-Aqqad, the writer.

"No," he said, "he's from the family of al-Aqqad the musician." I didn't understand the reference. "He was the best Egyptian qanun player ever. He played for Umm Kulthum in the 1930s."

The Ustaz knew all the old qanun players. He used to play it himself when he was young. It was his favorite oriental instrument. Through his great love of music he'd managed to enroll in the Institute of Arab Music while he was studying philosophy at the Faculty of Arts. At that time he was thinking seriously of becoming a professional musician. His teacher of the instrument at the institute was the grandson of al-Aqqad, who'd played for Umm Kulthum. The dean of the institute was Muhammad al-Aqqad Bey, also one of the al-Aqqad family.

The Ustaz related to me that in order to join the institute he had first to meet the dean and get his approval. The Ustaz had entered the office of Muhammad al- Aqqad Bey, in awe of the occasion.

The Ustaz went on: "Al-Aqqad Bey looked me up and down and asked, 'Why are you so old?' I explained that I had not just completed secondary school but that I was already a student in the third year at university and loved music. He asked me which instrument I preferred.

"'The qanun,' I said, whereupon he snorted coarsely in a way that filled me with embarrassment.

"I winced and my face turned red, imagining that the man didn't like the instrument. He then gave me an application form to fill in and while I was doing so he kept looking at me, snorting from time to time. I was so embarrassed I didn't know what to do. After I'd left the room I saw a friend who was a student in the institute and who'd come with me to present my papers.

"'I've abandoned the idea of registering at the institute,' I said and told him what al-Aqqad Bey had done.

"My friend laughed: 'I should have warned you that the man has a congenital problem with his throat, which makes him snort without meaning to!'

I couldn't control my laughter but the Ustaz hadn't finished yet.

"I wasn't persuaded by this explanation," he said. "It seemed to me that the dean of the institute was making fun of me, until the musician Abd al-Halim Nuweira told me something that convinced me my friend was right. He said that at the opening of the institute al-Aqqad Bey had decided to perform in the orchestra that would play the national anthem in the presence of King Fouad. Everyone had tried to persuade him to change his mind, fearing that he'd make that noise in front of the king, who would take offense at them all. According to Abd al-Halim Nuweira, however, al-Aqqad Bey was absolutely determined to play in front of the king and promised them he wouldn't breathe while the king was in the audience. The reception went off well but as soon as the king had left al-Aqqad ran backstage and did it as loudly as possible, like someone who'd been holding his breath for the whole time that the king was present!"

We both laughed and then he said, "Anyway, every time I met al-Aqqad in the institute I felt embarrassed about what had happened. I didn't relax until I left the institute a year later with top grades. I wasn't able to manage both the institute and my university studies."

"How did the man get into your room?" I asked.

"It seems he was visiting a relative in the room next door and he asked to see me. I told them to let him in."

At that point the doctors arrived to do their morning check-up and found us laughing. "You don't know what you've missed!" I said, in response to their quizzical looks.

Five

"How did this happen?" I asked. "Wasn't there anyone with him in the room?"

I'd entered the Ustaz's room and found him asleep, with new bruises on his face. When I tried to speak to him he didn't answer. I hurried out to ask the doctors what had happened. One of them met me as he was coming into the room to do the temperature, blood pressure, and other regular tests.

"He fell out of bed last night," he said.

"He fell out?" I said. "What do you mean, he fell out?"

"I wasn't there," he replied, "but they told me he fell out of bed last night."

I went back in with the doctor. The Ustaz was still asleep with the medical equipment around him showing his heartbeat and the level of oxygen in his blood, while his breathing rate showed on a screen above the bed.

"These machines weren't here yesterday!" I said to the doctor.

"We've turned the room into an intensive care unit," he replied, "so he'll get maximum care."

This reassured me a little, but the sight of those machines connected by wires and tubes to his body gave me no comfort. The day before,

Naguib Mahfouz was just as we'd known him before he'd entered the hospital. I'd been talking to him as if we'd been having one of our weekly sessions in the reception room of his home, but today he was a patient surrounded by medical equipment, with bruises on his face, unable to hear or answer me.

His being asleep was not normal. The Ustaz was orderly in everything—during the day he would sleep only after he'd had his lunch, at around two. So why was he asleep now? And he was always a light sleeper—any noise would wake him up immediately. But now he seemed to have lost consciousness completely. He didn't even notice me talking with the doctor.

"Is he drugged?" I asked.

"A little sedated," he replied, "just to give him some rest."

It was almost a week since he'd entered the hospital and this was the first time I hadn't talked with him or heard his jokes and his cheerful stories. When the doctor left, I sat beside the bed, listening despondently to his breathing.

He'd been expected to be discharged that day or the next. When would he be able to leave now?

Ten minutes went by without either of us moving. Those ten minutes seemed like hours.

I began to panic and rushed out of the room. The guards who I used to greet outside his home whenever I visited him had been transferred outside the hospital room.

One of them was new. Maybe he was an extra brought into the hospital.

"What's happened?" I asked them.

"He fell," they said—the same damned answer I received whenever I asked about him.

"What do you mean, he fell?"

They told me what I already knew and what I didn't want to hear: "He fell out of bed during the night."

My God, couldn't anyone say anything else?!

I left the hospital in a state of complete depression. When I reached my office at *al-Ahram* my colleague Mona Ragab called me anxiously. "They say the Ustaz has fallen over again."

I repeated to her the same damned statement that I hated to hear: "He fell out of bed during the night." But then I imagined the effect that this news would have on our readers if she published it the next morning, so I added quickly, "But he's fine now and there's no need to worry. It's better not to print anything in case it's misunderstood. Falling out of bed is just an accident that doesn't have any impact on his condition." (I wonder, was I trying to spare the readers their worries or was I trying to reassure myself?)

No more than half an hour had gone by before a journalist called to ask if it was true that the Ustaz had fallen down again in the hospital.

"He tripped over, like we all do sometimes," I replied. "Can't anyone trip over? It doesn't matter whether he fell or not. What matters is how he is and according to the doctors he's fine."

The calls kept coming. My God! How did the news spread so fast and who was spreading it? "I'm from *al-Hayat* newspaper. Is it true that our great novelist has had a fall in the hospital?" "I'm a correspondent from the German news agency. Has the Ustaz had another fall?'

"No, it's not true. He hasn't had a fall." I switched off my mobile.

In the afternoon I passed by the hospital. The doctor on duty told me, "There's no cause for alarm. We've just done an MRI scan. The fall didn't do any damage."

I went up to his room. He was still asleep. I sat with Madame Atiyatallah, who was also very down but not agitated.

"He was awake just now," she said.

"Did he say anything?" I asked.

"Not much," she replied. "He wouldn't eat. The doctors say it's the effect of the drug and that he'll get his appetite back when he comes off it."

We sat in silence, watching him as he slept. Occasionally he lifted his hand and opened his mouth and I imagined that he was awake and wanting to say something, but then his hand would drop again and he'd say nothing.

"How did he fall?" I asked again. "He's used to having a big bed at home," she said. "It's a double bed, you know, not a single like they have in hospitals."

I saw that they'd now put metal barriers on the sides of the bed, so that he wouldn't fall out again. It reminded me of a child's cot. Do we become children again when we get older?

One of the nurses came in and began speaking to him loudly. It was as if she was talking to a child: "Come on, we've got to wake up. The doctor said we have to get out of bed a bit today."

No response. There was no child in the room to answer her. The nurse lifted the high side of the bed and sat the Ustaz up. No response. "Just for a bit, then I'll come back." She left the room.

After a while Faten arrived. I asked her about Hoda. She said she was feeling a bit unwell. She'd been there the previous day. They'd been rotating their visits. Each would come for a while and then go home, when the other would come. As for Madame Atiyatallah, she stayed where she was, on her chair in the room, only leaving to go home in the evening.

Some doctors entered the room—three of them, followed by nurses and hospital administrators.

"How are you now, Naguib Bey?" shouted the senior one in his face.

They knew he was hard of hearing, but this shouting would always sound distorted to him and he wouldn't be able to hear anything. You have to speak into his left ear where he can hear, loudly and clearly, without shouting. I showed them how to do it, without commenting on the doctor's shouting—maybe they would realize anyway or maybe the Ustaz would hear and answer me. But it seemed that neither they nor he realized anything. He simply opened his eyes and then closed them again, as if he hadn't found anything worth looking at!

"Madame Atiyatallah said he'd been awake not long ago," I said. "But I found him asleep this morning and again now."

"We want to wake him up," they said.

One of them started shouting again, without coming close to his left ear: "Look, Mr. Salmawy's come to see you!"

He opened his eyes and closed them again, just like before.

"He's responding, which is good," said the senior one. Then he began looking at the numbers moving on the screen above the bed, and commented, "Good, good."

I waited till he'd finished and then I asked, "How is he?"

"Nothing to worry about," he said. "He just needs some rest and he'll be back to normal. We should cut down on the visits a little."

"The only ones who come are Mr. Salmawy, Mr. al-Ghitani, and Mr. al-Qa'id," said his wife. "He calls them his boys."

"It's important that he knows they're here with him," said the doctor. "Psychologically." Then he left, followed by all those that surrounded him.

The Ustaz hadn't been blessed with any sons. Umm Kulthum was the eldest of his daughters, followed by Fatma. However, Umm Kulthum had not been the first child. Before her, Naguib Mahfouz had fathered a son, but his wife had discovered during the pregnancy that the baby had died without her knowing and without the doctor who was treating her knowing either. Every time he'd given her a check-up he'd said, "Good, good, you're both doing fine." The baby had died when she'd been hit by a bike on a street in Alexandria. The doctor had given her an injection to keep the embryo in the womb, but after a while the truth emerged, followed by the dead embryo. The mother had begun a long course of treatment to overcome the effects of losing the baby. She was not blessed with another baby for two years, when Umm Kulthum came into the world. The Ustaz gave the girl the name that meant the most to him in the world of music, the Star of the East who for decades had filled the lives of the Arab people with joy and beauty, just as he had in the world of literature. They had both become icons for their nation and symbols of its achievements in literature and art.

After Umm Kulthum came Fatma, which was the name of Naguib Mahfouz's mother—as well as the title of one of the singer Umm Kulthum's most popular films. They were two unblemished flowers who inherited from him all of his noble characteristics, from the gentleness of his nature to his modesty and good company; and they were later destined, despite their aversion to spectacle and the limelight, to appear before the whole world under the brightest spotlight, when they stood before the King of Sweden, Carl Gustav II, to receive the world's highest literary award on behalf of their father.

It seems that Naguib Mahfouz, who had lost his unborn son, had decided to father all the sons of his country in compensation. And this is how he dealt with his nearest and dearest—he often consulted me about how to help someone who was in need, as if he were speaking about his own son: "I want to get him a job in a respectable place," he'd say, or, "Try to publish this story of his somewhere."

Even though I'd known the Ustaz since the 1970s I got to know his daughters well only when I managed to persuade him that they should accompany me to Sweden for the Nobel celebrations, for which he had chosen me to represent him. While I delivered Mahfouz's speech in the Swedish Academy, it was Umm Kulthum and Fatma who received the prize from the hands of the King.

The Ustaz lifted his left hand, which was stretched out beside him on the bed, and Faten took it in her own hands without speaking.

I felt that he was holding onto his daughter's hand. I looked at the peaceful smile that had spread on Faten's face and I remembered her and Hoda's faces when they'd received the Nobel prize from the King. Hoda's face had the features of the Ustaz while Faten's had his spirit. They both had such beautiful smiles on their faces when they approached the King—it was Naguib Mahfouz's features and his spirit, combined in two girls who captured the hearts of those assembled at that solemn ceremony on the stage in Stockholm on 10 December 1988. After that, every time I saw Hoda and Faten smiling I remembered that occasion, even when Hoda had put on the *higab* in 2001 and Faten had done the same three years later.

A few moments went by, before being interrupted by a stream of phone calls from people asking after the Ustaz. Madame Atiyatallah continued to answer them patiently and politely. Later, as I was leaving, I asked the hospital not to transfer these calls to his room, since most of them were from people we didn't know.

"They say the effect of the sedative will wear off tomorrow," I told Faten.

"God be with him," she replied.

Six

I picked up the newspapers and went to the hospital. I was planning to read him some of the news. I looked for something that wasn't depressing but couldn't find anything. Israel had committed a terrible atrocity in Qana, in southern Lebanon, equal to the first atrocity there in 1996, and the U.S.A was still obstructing progress toward a ceasefire. What could I tell him? I left the papers in the car.

The Ustaz had regained consciousness, but although sometimes he spoke to us at other times he was distant, as if he was still under the effect of the sedative.

This was not the first time he'd returned to the Police Hospital since the attack in 1994. In February 2003 he'd been struck by a severe cold and bronchitis, accompanied by pains in the stomach and a general weakness. His doctors had advised him to go into intensive care, where he was put on drips to overcome the dehydration caused by the rise in his temperature. But this time it was different. On the two previous occasions Mahfouz's smile had never left him, nor the lightheartedness with which he'd greet his guests but which he was now starting to lose for the first time since I'd met him at the beginning of the 1970s.

I was at that time still in the prime of life and had a good relationship with Tawfiq al-Hakim. I used to finish my work as a foreign affairs editor on the fourth floor of *al-Ahram* as quickly as possible in order to go up to his office on the sixth floor, where I'd often meet writers and intellectuals. In al-Hakim's office I got to meet Tharwat Abaza, Dr. Hussein Fawzi, Dr. Bint al-Shati', as well as Dr. Louis Awad and the artist Salah Taher whom I knew already. That was where I first met Naguib Mahfouz. It was usually just a normal greeting, consisting of no more than a hello accompanied by his famous smile. We took part in the meetings along with everyone else, without any special communication between the two of us.

In 1983 I received from the printer the proofs of a collection of stories I'd written, bound together in the form of a book inside a cover proof. I decided to give this copy to Naguib Mahfouz who had, a few months before, given me a copy of his new novel *One Hour Remains*. Inside the book I wrote something to the effect that this copy was distinguished from the copies I would give to other people when the book came out. But I was surprised a few days later when the copy I'd given him came back to me. What had I done? Had I overstepped the mark by giving him a proof rather than the book itself? I flicked through the book quickly and to my surprise found some lines on the last page that read, "I took the liberty of writing a few suggestions for you on this text, but I wrote them in pencil so if you don't like them you can rub them out . . . Sincerely, Naguib Mahfouz."

When I'd given him the book I hadn't imagined that he would read it. I was amazed that he had not only read it but also offered his comments and returned it, so that I could make use of the comments before going to press, or even rub them out if I wished!

But who could erase something written by the hand of Naguib Mahfouz? I implemented all his suggestions, just as he wrote them, astonished that this giant had not hesitated to stoop to offer a helping hand to a young man at the beginning of his literary career.

From that time my relationship with Naguib Mahfouz grew stronger and he came to occupy a special place for me after he'd given me his unrequested time and attention. Nevertheless, when Tawfiq al-Hakim died in the summer of 1987 I stopped going up to the sixth floor of the building. My direct contact with Naguib Mahfouz came to a stop for a while, until I was taken by surprise at the end of the following year when he chose me to be his representative at the Nobel prize ceremony in Sweden.

Suddenly the Ustaz woke up and spoke but we couldn't understand what he was saying. His voice was clear but what he said was not comprehensible. He said it again. We couldn't understand. He stopped talking and didn't say any more.

I left the room. There was a sharp chill in the air from the strength of the air conditioning. How could the man put up with this arctic temperature? I looked for one of the hospital workers.

"The air in the room is very cold," I said.

The man hurried into the room and said, "We'll turn the air conditioning off."

"Why turn it off?" I said. I couldn't understand.

Is the inability to work equipment a part of our culture? We seem to imagine that air conditioning was invented in order to bring us the climate from the North Pole. If you go to a cinema or any public place you come out with a cold, even though any air conditioner can be adjusted to the required temperature. The point about air conditioners is not to freeze the air but to maintain a natural temperature in both summer and winter.

The man turned the air conditioning off and left the room. Just a few minutes later the temperature started to rise again, so they turned the air conditioning back on!

Madame Atiyatallah suggested, "Why don't we open the window instead—it looks over the Nile." When we did this a gentle breeze blew in from the great river that the Ustaz loved so much.

He spoke again. His words were clear this time even if he was a little slow. "How are you feeling now, Ustaz Naguib?" I asked.

He was silent for a bit and then said, "I don't know. You tell me."

"The doctors say you're right as rain."

He smiled for the first time without saying anything.

No doubt he was remembering how we'd used to joke about Tawfiq al-Hakim when we'd visited him in the Arab Contractors Hospital in Gebel Asfar—he'd called the doctors "the rain doctors" because every time he'd asked them how he was they'd say, "You're right as rain."

"Don't you want anything to eat?" I asked. He indicated with his hand that he didn't.

"They say you don't eat anything at all. But food restores the body."

It was a while before he said, "I don't feel like it."

I tried to talk to him about a few topics but I felt I was talking to myself. No one answered me and maybe no one even heard me. Yusif al-Qa'id arrived.

"Yusif al-Qa'id's here," I said.

He greeted al-Qa'id and then he wasn't there any more. Where did he go? We didn't know. We sat in the room with Madame Atiyatallah. Al-Qa'id had brought a lot of news which he related in a long monologue.

After a while the Ustaz looked at us and said, "I don't want to put you to any more trouble."

Al-Qa'id said to me, "Maybe he wants to rest."

"Let's give him some quiet then," I said and took al-Qa'id out of the room.

When I passed by the next day they had inserted tubes into his neck because he still wasn't eating. He'd also refused to get out of bed since he'd fallen out on that unfortunate night. Madame Atiyatallah told me that when she'd arrived that morning, leaning on her walking stick, the first thing he'd said to her was, "Mind you don't fall."

The barber arrived. The doctor had said that this would refresh him and improve his mood but the Ustaz refused to leave his bed. So the barber shaved him in bed and took a photo of him. A few days later some magazines published the picture that the barber had taken, with the bruises on Mahfouz's face after the fall. Everyone saw the picture of the great writer in his pyjamas, with the bruises on his forehead and right cheek, but his mood—which was the reason for the barber's visit—had not improved.

"Would you like to drink some juice?" I asked. He indicated that he wouldn't. "You don't have to eat," I said. "Just drink something—milk or even water. The doctor said your body has to be active." He showed again that he didn't want anything.

Every one of his refusals cut me like a knife.

"What can we do?" I asked the doctor.

"He'll stay on a drip until he starts eating again," he replied.

That evening Gamal al-Ghitani phoned me to suggest that we divide up our visits—the two of us and Yusif al-Qa'id—with one day each, so that we didn't leave him without a visitor for a day. Gamal knew that the Ustaz could not survive away from people and now that he'd been completely banned from having friends to visit it was necessary that any time he opened his eyes he'd find one of us beside him. I said I'd been going every day and would continue to do so.

"Something in your voice worries me," said Gamal.

"I *am* worried," I said.

"Me too," said Gamal, "but let's be optimistic."

The next day they informed me that his kidneys were not working properly but when I went in to see him he was conscious. I had with me this time a copy of the French magazine *Le Figaro*.

"Do you remember that French journalist who came last month and we promised him an article about the Dreams?" I asked him. Without waiting for a reply I added, "Here's the article, published in the latest edition of the magazine. I've brought you a copy."

"What does it say?" he asked.

"It's written in your words: *Old age constrains me, but I still have the freedom of my dreams!*... It's a whole page, with a very nice introduction."

"My thanks to them," he said.

"They are the ones thanking you for the article, with a kind letter and five copies of the magazine."

He didn't respond.

"There'll be an item on page one of tomorrow's *al-Ahram* about the article."

No response.

The eye specialist came in with new glasses, which he said might help improve the Ustaz's spirit.

"The doctor's brought you new glasses, Ustaz Naguib," I said.

"What's wrong with my old ones?" he asked.

"The old ones are fine," said the doctor, "but these are new." The doctor removed the old ones from the Ustaz's eyes and replaced them with the new ones.

"I'm very grateful," said the Ustaz with great politeness. After the doctor had gone the Ustaz said he couldn't see very well with the new glasses and asked me to take them off and put on the old ones.

After a while a different doctor came in. "How's the diarrhea?" he asked.

"A bit better," the nurse replied,

"How can he have diarrhea when he's not eating anything?" I asked.

"His digestive system isn't working well because of his refusal to eat," the doctor replied.

"It may be because of all the antibiotics we've given him with the drips," added a different doctor.

I sat in the waiting room with Hoda, who was amazed at how people deal with the elderly as if they're children. Most of the nurses spoke to him like a little child: "Come on now, eat up!" But what worried her more were the diapers they kept putting on him.

"Maybe it's because of the diarrhea," I said.

"But it's telling him that he's not able to control himself," she said. "And I know he can't accept that easily."

Seven

One of the Ustaz's close friends called me. "This has gone on too long. Every Monday we say next Monday we'll see him in the café as usual. But next Monday never comes. And we can't visit him in the hospital. Some of us have tried more than once, but we're never able to see him."

"He's going through a crucial stage," I said, "but it's not dangerous. Often he's asleep and doesn't see or speak to anyone."

The friend said, "For how long?"

"Pray that it doesn't go on too long," I said.

"What used to keep him in touch with life were his friends," said the friend. "If he's cut off from them and can't see them any more or listen to their stories and comment on them, he'll feel he's been cut off from life."

Psychologist Yahya al-Rakhawi had alerted us to the importance of the Ustaz's interaction with his friends after the assassination attempt in 1994—he'd noticed that the thing that could hurt Naguib Mahfouz most, he who'd spent his whole life surrounded by people, was if he were to withdraw into himself. So Dr. al-Rakhawi had arranged that once a week he could meet all those who wanted to see him, and had immediately set up a weekly meeting to take place every Friday. As a result, the Ustaz had gradually started to see the rest of his former friends, those whom he called the Harafish. This was on Thursday evenings, at the home of the director Tawfiq Salih, the only one of the Harafish who was still alive—with the exception of the relative newcomer, the artist Gamil Shafik—now that all the others had all passed away: Adel Kamil, Ahmad Zaki Makhluf, Muhammad Afifi, the actor Ahmad Mazhar, Amin al-Zahabi, Thabet Amin, Mahmud Shabana, Farid Amin, Asim Hilmi, and some of the more transient ones like Salah Jahin, Mustafa Mahmud, Louis Awad, and Ahmad Bahaa al-Din.

Some people think that all of Naguib Mahfouz's friends were part of the Harafish. But Mahfouz himself used this name only for the original group. He told me that Ahmad Mazhar was the originator of this name, which means—according to Mahfouz—the 'jerboas'! The rest of his friends were divided into groups who did not really mix. In fact there was some dissension between the various groups, who were united only by their close friendship with Naguib Mahfouz.

Besides the Thursdays, when the Harafish used to meet up, there was the Friday group with Dr. Yahya al-Rakhawi; Saturdays were dedicated to me; and on Sundays the Ustaz would meet with a group of friends at the Shepheard Hotel, including Dr. Muhammad al-Kafrawi, Ali Salem, and Ibrahim Abd al-Aziz. Mondays were spent in the coffee shop of the Novotel in Heliopolis and Tuesdays on the Farah Boat in Giza, where he'd meet with Gamal al-Ghitani, Yusif al-Qa'id, Abd al-Rahman al-Abnoudi and others. On Wednesdays he'd meet friends at the Sofitel in Maadi.

I didn't used to attend any of the meetings unless there was a special occasion, such as Naguib Mahfouz's birthday or if I had a foreign journalist with me who was visiting and wanted to record Mahfouz meeting his friends. I used to notice that he'd always ask about anyone who was missing: "So Gamal hasn't come today?" or "Hey, where's al-Kafrawi?"

For these reasons I knew that for the Ustaz the greatest pain in the hospital was not physical as much as psychological, being forced to miss his meetings with his friends and the daily routines that he always followed.

I entered the room and found it cold again. The doctors were gathered around his bed. He seemed to be awake, so I thanked God and waited until they'd finished their check-up before asking them how he was. They said he was stable but that it was still early to speak of any progress. He was still refusing to eat but he'd drunk a little water. I asked about his kidneys.

"They're more or less under control," they said, "but eating will help to restore them fully. The sooner he eats, the better—his blood acidity has risen due to their not functioning properly."

My God! How kind Tawfiq al-Hakim's doctors had been! Why could these doctors not just have said "As right as rain," instead of all these worrying details?

The doctors went out and I sat beside the Ustaz with a smile on my face, which did not convey what the doctors had said; it gave the impression that everything was fine.

"*Dreams in the Time of Convalescence* has finally been printed," I said, "and tomorrow I'll get the first copy off the press to bring to you."

He looked interested and said, "How much will it cost?"

"I didn't ask—the important thing is that it's out."

"The important thing is that people can afford it."

"Don't worry about people now," I said. "I'll find out the price and tell you when I come tomorrow."

Some nurses came in to check his temperature and other indicators on the screen above his bed; one of them said his temperature had gone up.

I asked him, "How much was your first book, Ustaz Naguib?"

I'd heard the story from him already but I wanted to continue our conversation. I was very worried that if we stopped talking he would lose consciousness again.

"You know how much it was," he said.

"I've forgotten."

"One piaster," he said. The nurses smiled and left what they were doing to gather round his bed and listen to him eagerly. It seemed as if their eagerness to hear his story encouraged him to speak and he went on: "The first novel I wrote was *Mockery of the Fates*."

"And how much did you get for it?" I asked.

"It wasn't money," he said. "It was five hundred copies of the book!"

"What did you do with them?"

"I put them on a horse-drawn carriage and took them to the first bookstore I came across. I showed them to the owner and told him I didn't know what to do with them. The owner took pity on me and took the books at the price I mentioned and said he'd pay me for each copy as and when he sold it."

With his reminiscences Naguib Mahfouz spread an atmosphere of joy in the room, despite the pain he was suffering from his deteriorating kidneys, the acidity of his blood, the rise in his temperature, his diarrhea, and his periodic loss of consciousness.

Trying to keep the conversation going, I asked, "Did you get your money in the end?"

He didn't reply, so one of the nurses said, "Mister Salmawy's asking if you got your money."

"He knows the whole story," he said.

"But *we* don't know," said the nurse.

"For months I used to pop into the bookstore, imagining I'd get a few piasters for what he'd sold, but it didn't happen. After a while I couldn't find my book on the shelf so I thought maybe he'd sold them all. But then I discovered that the owner had stored the whole lot away. 'There's no market for them,' he said."

All the nurses laughed and I laughed too, but the story wasn't over. The Ustaz carried on in the midst of our laughter: "A few years later my novel *Khan al-Khalili* was published and was selling well. By chance I was passing the bookstore when suddenly I saw *Mockery of the Fates* on display at a new price. When the owner saw me he said, 'I owe you some money.' And he actually paid me, but based on the original price that we'd agreed—just one piaster!"

As the nurses laughed I felt they wanted to listen to more stories. "Do you know the price of the Ustaz's latest book?" I asked. They were eager to hear the answer, so I told them: "Five thousand dollars!" They gasped.

In late 2005 I came back from a trip to America and went to visit the Ustaz with an unusual book. It was fifteen inches square and priced at five thousand dollars. It was Mahfouz's novel, *Arabian Nights and Days*, which he'd first published in Arabic in 1982. The new edition was published by the New York-based Limited Editions Club, a publisher that specializes in *livres d'artiste*, or artistic books. Their books are usually by renowned writers such as Cavafy, Rilke, and Mallarmé, and illustrated with original pictures by leading artists. They are printed on hand-made paper and individually sewn.

Limited Editions had wanted to publish a novel by Naguib Mahfouz and asked the Ustaz to recommend one. I conveyed the request to Mahfouz, who suggested a choice between *The Harafish* and *Arabian Nights and Days*. The publishers chose the latter. They then asked him to suggest an Egyptian artist to illustrate it and he proposed Nazli Madkour. They also asked me to write an introduction but I responded that I couldn't possibly introduce someone like Naguib Mahfouz. Instead I wrote an epilogue.

The launch was held at the Corcoran Museum in Washington D.C. Every copy of the limited edition came in a box made of raw silk lined with velvet and was signed by both the author and artist.

Back in Cairo I presented the book to Mahfouz. "Here is your new book," I said.

"That's quite something!" he replied, laughing at the luxurious item. "How much does it cost?"

"Five thousand dollars, or around 30,000 Egyptian pounds," I answered.

"God help us," he gasped.

"He did," I said. "The book has almost sold out!"

"At that price?" he asked.

"Yes," I answered. "From one piaster, the price of your first book, to five thousand dollars. Imagine that!"

"Well, the piaster was a good start," said Mahfouz.

When the doctor came in, everyone in the room was laughing. "That's good," the young doctor said, "That's the Naguib Mahfouz we're used to. Now he just needs to eat."

The food was ready and the doctor made a great effort to try to persuade the Ustaz to eat, taking advantage of the joyful atmosphere that he had created.

"It's me who'll feed you today," the doctor told him.

"Don't trouble yourself," the Ustaz replied politely. "I'm not hungry at the moment."

"I want to tell people that today I fed Naguib Mahfouz with my own hands," said the doctor. "Please allow me this honor."

The Ustaz's face showed traces of embarrassment as he refused the food from the doctor. I remembered Hoda's words when she talked about how the elderly were treated like children.

His features began to lose their brightness as he closed his mouth and said, "You're feeding a dead man!"

Eight

The first copy of *Dreams in the Time of Convalescence* had reached me—I took it and set off for the hospital.

The elevator operator stopped at the second floor, so I said, "I'm going to room 612, upstairs, to Ustaz Naguib Mahfouz."

"He's left it," said the man. "He's in the intensive care unit."

I rushed out of the lift to the intensive care unit on the right. On the way I met Dr. Ibrahim Awadein coming out of the room and asked him, "Didn't you say you'd turned his own room upstairs into an intensive care unit?"

"Yes," he replied, "but he's caught bronchitis and his bronchial passages are blocked, causing him difficulty breathing, so we had to put him on artificial respiration for a while."

I went in and one of the doctors seemed to be beating him all over his body while the Ustaz was pleading: "Enough, I beg you, that's enough!"

This was the physiotherapist who was trying to stimulate and move his limbs while the Ustaz was barely conscious and aware only that someone was beating him all over for no apparent reason! The physiotherapist removed the sheet covering him and started to bend his leg and straighten it out, like a manual water pump that was not managing to bring water up from within the earth.

The Ustaz kept saying, very quietly, "I beg you!" removing the physiotherapist's hand from his leg and covering it up again, at which point the physiotherapist would try again. The doctor reached the chest and began knocking with his hands on the area around the heart, as if he wanted to activate it and prevent it from stopping.

The Ustaz cried out without losing his composure, "Please, please leave me alone! Why are you doing this to me?"

I quickly bent down to his left ear so that he could hear me. "That's the physiotherapy, Ustaz Naguib. Just a few minutes and it'll be over." But he didn't hear me.

It's really strange how a person can speak without being conscious, telling people he cannot see to stop beating him, without being able to hear what's said to him in his ear or to answer it.

I said to the doctor, "That's enough for now."

"The session's not over yet," he said, "but we can come back later. Maybe by then he'll be awake and more prepared for the treatment."

As soon as they'd left, a young woman doctor came in carrying a new hearing aid for his ear. No one had asked them to change his hearing aid but apparently the hospital managers felt that Naguib Mahfouz's presence there required that doctors of all kinds should come along to carry out all possible treatments. This was their way of showing their care for their special patient. His family often expressed their gratitude to them and every time we talked to the press I conveyed thanks from all of us to the hospital management and its doctors, as well as to the doctors brought in from outside the hospital—like the famous Dr. Hossam Muwafi, one of the top specialists in critical cases, who took responsibility for Ustaz Naguib's case when he went into intensive care—and the other doctors who supervised him from the moment he entered the hospital.

The young doctor removed the old hearing aid from the Ustaz's ear and inserted in its place the new one that she'd brought. When the new device started emitting a whistle that bothered the Ustaz, she pushed it further in and the whistling stopped. As soon as she took her hand off it started whistling again. It was clear from the Ustaz's expression that it was really bothering him, even though he was unconscious.

I tried to dissuade the doctor from putting the device in: "It seems to need a bit of adjusting," I said.

"It only makes this noise when it's not fitted properly in the ear," she said. "If it's in properly, the noise will stop."

I didn't say anything more, while the doctor continued without success to try to adjust the device. Finally I said, "It's obvious that the noise is troubling him. Why don't we leave it for a bit until he wakes up and then try again?" She agreed, took out the device and was putting the old one in again when I noticed that his ear was scratched inside, possibly from the old hearing aid, which had never been taken out even when he was asleep. It may have been rubbing and causing the skin to peel off. But since he was suffering from diabetes, this—as far as I knew—would not help the wound, superficial though it was, to heal quickly.

I told the doctor, "Why don't we take the hearing aid out completely since he's asleep now?" (I noticed that I was avoiding using the word "coma.")

"Yes,' she said, "that would be better."

The doctor gave the hearing aid to the nurse who put it in the drawer of the bedside table. As soon as she'd left I removed his glasses too and gave them to the nurse so that they could not scratch him either. "When he wakes up he'll ask for them," I told her. The nurse put the glasses in the drawer with the hearing aid.

I took out the copy of *Dreams in the Time of Convalescence* that he had been waiting for. The cover was nicely done, with one of Naguib Mahfouz's best photographs. It was the famous picture of him sitting quietly with his hand resting on his stick. The picture bore all the hallmarks of his character: calm, tolerance, and goodness, as well as strength, firmness, and pride. The picture had been taken by the French photographer Gilles Perrin for the cover of my book *Mon Egypte*, which included my conversation with Mahfouz and which was published in France in 1996 by Éditions Lattès. The book had won the *Prix de la Société des Gens de Lettres* for that year.

I looked at the photo of the Ustaz on the cover and then at the face lying on the pillow of the hospital bed. How many years had gone by since this photo had been taken? Exactly ten. And how many years since he'd entered the hospital just a month ago? It seemed as if another decade had taken its toll since that Saturday when I'd met him in his home, just a few hours before he fell over in his bedroom. But the picture on the cover of the book was the original, the real likeness, while the face lying in front of me on the pillow was not that of Naguib Mahfouz. Rather it was the face of time or the face of the cursed illness that came from I don't know where, just a month after he'd been standing waving goodbye from the door of his apartment, saying he'd be waiting for me the following Saturday.

What should I do? He'd been patiently waiting for this book in his old age, when the joys of life had become so few. Now that it was published, and in my hands, what was I to do with it?

I would come back with it the next day—maybe I'd find him conscious and I could speak to him and describe the book to him and tell him that they'd put his picture, my picture, on the cover.

Nine

When I went in the next day his voice was strong and his words clear, but all he said were two words, "O God! O God!" He kept repeating them while the doctors tried to place an oxygen mask over his face. Each time they tried, he removed the mask.

I realized that although he wasn't conscious, he was reacting to the attempts to put the damned mask on. He must have thought it was some kind of muzzle. He removed it and started saying again, "O God! O God!"

He wasn't aware of our presence; he was simply reacting to the annoyance caused by the oxygen mask.

I noticed that the number of drips had increased. His left hand was swollen from the needle that was inserted into his vein.

They noticed this too and moved the needle from his left hand to his right, the hand with which he had penned so many marvels over a period of almost seventy years of writing. This was also the hand that had suffered partial disablement after the attempt on his life, which for a while paralyzed his arm from the neck to the fingers. After that incident he was able to use his hand only with great care. The physiotherapy lasted for more than a year, so any photo from that time shows him carefully holding his right hand in his left. And now here he was, with needles and tubes inserted into the veins of both hands. Maybe his unconsciousness was for the best, so that he wasn't able to see what had happened to his right hand, the one the Brazilian writer Paolo Coelho had bent to kiss in front of us as soon as he'd entered the room, before saying with humility and respect: "This is the hand that wrote some of the greatest literary masterpieces people have ever read."

Come now Paolo, and see what we have done to that hand. Come and see how swollen it is, its color turned dark in a way I cannot describe, a mixture of crimson red and dark blue. You have kissed it but we have done with it what you could not imagine and will not see; and before that there were those lunatics who attacked him in his neck with a knife, whose poison spread to the very tips of the fingers of this same right hand.

For a long time after the attack the Ustaz wasn't capable of using his right hand. He had a stock of short stories that he sent to *Nisf al-dunya* magazine in time for its regular publication date, but he needed to be able to use his right hand for other things like signing bank papers and contracts.

One day I was surprised to hear him say, "I want you to make me a signet ring that I can use until my hand gets better. I can't ask anyone else to make me such a ring that I'll use to sign everything." I was amazed that the greatest writer in the Arab world should have to use a seal, like simple people who do not read or write!

I had to ask around to find someone to make such a ring without letting them know why I was asking. My inquiries led me to a ring maker in Muhammad Ali Street where I went in person, since I could not entrust a messenger with such a mission.

The ring maker was most surprised when I asked him to make me a signet ring bearing the name of Naguib Mahfouz. The man looked at me in astonishment but he quickly grasped the situation. "It's just a similar name," he said. He then clapped one hand over the other and added, "God be praised! . . . Two Naguib Mahfouzes! One of them's an international writer and the other one doesn't even know how to write his own name!"

The manager of the Bank Misr branch was even more surprised when I asked him to replace the authorized signature of Ustaz Naguib Mahfouz with the impression of the ring that I'd brought with me.

But thanks to the physiotherapy and his persistent practice, it was only a few months before the Ustaz was able to use his hand again and start signing for the bank and writing as usual.

I looked at his right hand, punctured by needles, and told myself it was a temporary crisis, that the glorious hand would soon be able to revert to its former state that the whole world knew so well.

The Ustaz lifted up his left hand as if talking to a crowd of people. He looked like the statue of Saad Zaghloul, carved by Egypt's late pioneer sculptor Mahmud Mukhtar. Mukhtar had been right to enlarge the hand of the statue as he had. It was the hand of an orator addressing the crowd. Now it was our novelist raising his hand to talk to us. The hand of Saad was solid, its fingers splayed, while the hand of the novelist was delicate, the fingers closed.

"He wants to say something," I said.

"What does he want to say?" they asked.

I had no reply. Whatever he wanted to say, it was not only meant for us here, standing around his hospital bed. Through us he seemed to be addressing all of humanity, those whom he had addressed over the years through his writings.

They placed the oxygen mask on his face once again, and he put out his hand and removed it again.

"Why does he need this mask?" I asked.

"He has a blockage in his bronchial tubes because he's not coughing," they said. "So he's not expelling any phlegm."

I learned that since the day before they'd been clearing phlegm from his chest mechanically. They said it was an extremely painful procedure. I thanked God that I hadn't been present. How could he have a bronchial blockage and still be able to talk so loudly and imploringly when he said, "O God, O God"?

Dr. Hossam Muwafi came in. "The oxygen mask is better than an artificial breathing apparatus," he told me, "which presents a risk of the lung adjusting and making it difficult afterward to wean him off it."

"What do you mean," I said, "wean him off it?"

"I mean, in the same way you wean a child off the breast. In both cases it's a procedure that should happen gradually."

Then the doctor changed the subject, saying that he'd arranged for daily press conferences at noon to brief the media on the latest developments regarding the Ustaz's health. He invited me to attend the conference with him in order to reassure people. "A doctor's statement will be more credible," I told him, "and anyway I need reassuring too."

After the doctor had left, one of the nurses noticed that the Ustaz's mouth needed a clean-up. He tried to clean it with a little wooden stick wrapped in cotton wool, like the ones doctors use to check a patient's throat. The Ustaz immediately shut his mouth. The nurse said, "He thinks we're trying to insert the instrument for removing the phlegm into his throat."

My God! It was my turn now to beseech Him to have mercy on all of us.

I remembered a conversation we'd had about ten years before, when he was eighty-five. He'd said he hoped that his end would be easy, that some people leave this life as if they're going on a picnic, without being aware that they were passing away, while others depart after a great struggle.

Then he related to me how two of his brothers had passed away in very different ways. One had had cancer and the last two weeks of his life had been a real ordeal, while the other had died while having tea with his son—his son had called to him and he hadn't replied.

But why do I talk about death while he is still alive? Has he not had bronchitis before this and been admitted to this very hospital just three years ago? And had they not inserted this same narrow tube into his hand? We'd been just as anxious then as we are now, but death didn't cross our minds, so why think about it now? He's still very much alive, still resisting the damned muzzle that they want to suppress his breathing with. Is this not a sign that he still holds onto life?

If he'd lost the will to live he would have let them do what they wanted, but he resisted. Each time he removed the oxygen mask my confidence grew that he would emerge from this crisis and leave the hospital as he had left before.

He was silent for a while and left the mask on his face. Was he asleep? Had he lost consciousness and was no longer aware of this suffocating muzzle, or was he simply no longer resisting? As though responding to my thoughts and showing me that he was still alive and resisting, he put out his hand again and removed the mask.

Well done, Ustaz! Take it off again!

"Tie his hands up!" the doctor said.

"Leave him alone!" I said to myself. "I beg you, leave him alone! Let him resist. Let him hold onto life. Don't break his will. Don't make him feel—as his daughter Hoda said—that he's no longer in control of his destiny."

They brought a strip of muslin and tied his hands to the metal frame of the bed. I searched for anything to justify them not tying his hands.

"Could that not prevent the circulation in his hands?" I suggested.

"No," they said.

They put the clear plastic mask on his face more easily this time, and there was no resistance. He tried to lift his hand to remove it but he wasn't able to.

"Leave him!" I said to myself again. "Maybe he'll lift his hand to tell us something like the hero of his youth, Saad Zaghloul."

He did try to raise his hand while it was tied to the bed. It rose just a few centimeters before falling to his side. He tried again and again without success, and finally gave in. He did not raise it again.

I went out into the waiting room. It was empty and for the first time since the Ustaz had entered the hospital I found myself crying.

Ten

When I entered the intensive care room I found Dr. Hossam Muwafi by the Ustaz's bed. I asked him for his personal assessment. "It's critical, no doubt, but not hopeless," the doctor replied. I didn't know whether to be happy or sad. His saying that the situation was critical was cause for concern. I'd lived through it personally day by day and knew how bad it was. But for him to give a formal diagnosis that the situation was critical, that was another matter. However, no matter how painful this description was, I was filled with hope by the doctor saying that the Ustaz's condition was not hopeless.

"So, there is hope," I said.

"Some patients in his condition have pulled through and led normal lives," he said.

The Ustaz was still asleep but I noticed that his glasses and hearing aid had been put back on. They said he'd asked for them. This meant that he'd been conscious. When was that, and why did it not happen while I was there? There was so much that I wanted to talk to him about. The nurse said he'd been awake now and then but when Dr. Muwafi tried to wake him up and said, "Naguib Bey, Mr. Salmawy's arrived," he neither heard nor answered.

Dr. Muwafi said his condition was still stable. "We just have to be patient and monitor the situation hourly, rather than daily."

I accompanied him to the lecture hall of the hospital, where the daily press conference was to take place, but found myself still unable to give assurances to anyone; so I made do simply by conveying thanks from the Ustaz's family and friends to the hospital management and the team of top doctors who'd been monitoring his condition. Then I added that I would now leave them to the head of the medical team, Dr. Hossam Muwafi, who would present the medical report about the great novelist's condition. I stepped down quickly from the podium in order to return to the Ustaz's bedside.

At the door of the hall I found more cameras waiting for me. One of the presenters from a satellite channel provoked me by asking about the controversial *Children of the Alley*, which had been the reason—according to him—for Naguib Mahfouz winning the Nobel prize!

"Who told you that?" I asked.

"It's well known," he said.

"It's not true. Firstly, the Nobel prize is not awarded for a particular work, but to a writer. Some prizes *are* given for individual books, like the Booker Prize in Great Britain, the Goncourt in France, or the Pulitzer in the United States, but not the Nobel prize. If it was awarded for a particular work, any young writer could win by submitting a good work of literature. But it's only given to great writers in recognition of their influence on humanity over a period of years, which cannot be limited to a single novel. Furthermore, the grounds for awarding the prize to Naguib Mahfouz are publicly known and there is no suggestion that he won the award for a single novel. The official communiqué of the Nobel committee mentions the most important of the novelist's works, including *Children of the Alley* as well as the *Cairo Trilogy* and other novels, so why should anyone say he won it because of *Children of the Alley*?"

Before the young presenter could reply to this rhetorical question I followed up: "Do you know when *Children of the Alley* was published?" He didn't answer. "In 1959," I replied. "The Ustaz won the Nobel prize in 1988, nearly 30 years later. If the Nobel prize had been awarded for this novel why did it happen three decades later?"

My answer seemed only to encourage the presenter to ask another question: "Other people say he won the Nobel prize because of his support for the Camp David agreement with Israel!"

"As if we don't believe that we have a writer who deserves the prize for the quality of his work," I said, "and we keep finding other non-literary reasons to explain why he won!"

Naguib Mahfouz deserved the prize for his work alone. In fact the award came so late that it had begun to damage the credibility of the prize itself. I myself had heard the former president of the Nobel committee, Sture Allén, say to Naguib Mahfouz in his office in *al-Ahram* newspaper: "Arabic literature has a great heritage that we had ignored for almost a century. You have repaired this injury!"

How could the head of the Nobel prize committee say this and yet we say, "No, he didn't deserve it—he must have won it for some other reason." What is this sense of inferiority to the world?

"But he *did* support Camp David!" said the presenter.

"He did *not* support Camp David," I said. "He called for peace. That's different. You'd be amazed if I told you that I don't think Naguib Mahfouz ever read the Camp David agreement and he often asked me about some of its clauses. So he never announced that he supported it or that he rejected it, for that matter. But he did announce both before and after the agreement that he was for peace and an end to bloodshed. If he had read it, then maybe he could support it or reject it, but he didn't. He supported peace—this is a humane attitude, not a political stand."

"What about the Palestinian cause?" the man asked.

"Naguib Mahfouz was one of the strongest supporters of the Palestinian cause. At a time when the agreed term was 'the legitimate rights of the Palestinian people' and no politician could even say the words 'Palestinian state,' Mahfouz chose the moment when the world's attention was focused on him, in his Nobel prize address, to call openly for a Palestinian state."

I felt that if I carried on answering all the presenter's questions this passing encounter would turn into a lengthy talk show, so I took leave from the presenter and went back to the Ustaz's room.

Eleven

The next day the Ustaz didn't wake up at all.

We kept waiting for a word or a gesture, but there was none. Every time I came in I could see only the machines and could hear only their monotonous ticking.

I sat with Madame Atiyatallah, looking through the morning papers. The headlines read, "Mahfouz regains consciousness: situation still critical," and "Great novelist's condition stable after temperature returns to normal."

"Did he actually wake up and ask for his glasses and his hearing aid?" I asked the Madame. "Yes," she replied, "but nothing more than that and he didn't speak again."

There was a small room—next to the one where he lay in the intensive care unit—which the hospital had equipped as a waiting room leading off from his. Madame Atiyatallah would often sit there when the doctors were in the Ustaz's room. She couldn't bear some of the medical procedures that he was subjected to from time to time. Yesterday the hospital manager noticed that this antechamber was unusually hot. Today I found they'd installed a new air conditioner there. I told her that I had conveyed her thanks to the hospital management and doctors during the press briefing the previous day, for all they had done. This made her happy.

I went back into his room; he was still asleep, just as we'd left him. I tried again: "How are you, Ustaz Naguib?"

His eyes flickered but he didn't answer. Did this mean he'd heard me or simply that my question was a disturbance like the whistling of the hearing aid? I decided that he had heard me and that he'd greeted me with a movement of his eyes. But there was nothing more.

I went out again to Madame Atiyatallah. Hoda and Faten had arrived. Faten told me that the day before, he'd said, "I want to go!"

"Did he recognize you?" I asked.

"I think so," she replied, "or maybe he thought I was one of the nurses."

"I don't think so," I said. "The nurses have a special deep green uniform. It stands out even with his sight." Even though he could not see details, he couldn't mistake that color.

"Then there's the *higab*," I added.

We sat discussing many things, spurred on by the hope that he would soon wake up and speak to us as he'd spoken the day before to Faten. We spoke about what Mahfouz's daughters were doing now that they'd left their jobs. Hoda had done media studies at the AUC, while Faten had studied business administration. Hoda had worked for a few years at Hughes, the international aviation company, while Faten had worked at Xerox until they'd both decided to stop working.

He'd certainly made a great effort the day before when he said, "I want to go!" But did he mean that he wanted to go home or that he simply wanted to go? It was just a word, and how could we know what he meant?

He loved the poetry of al-Mutanabbi and at that moment a line of the poet went through my mind:

Enough that you find death a remedy
And enough that fate be your wish.

Faten adjusted her *higab* and I asked, "What did the Ustaz think when you first put on the *higab*, the two of you?"

"He didn't say anything at all," she replied. "He must have thought it was a personal matter that only concerned us."

She paused and then added, "One day Hoda came in and he saw her head was covered and said, 'You've taken the *higab*?' She said yes. 'What about Faten?' he asked. 'No, she hasn't,' she said. And he didn't make any comment."

I told myself, "If he hadn't discussed their decisions to refuse proposals of marriage, would he question what they chose to wear, even if it was the *higab*?"

The Ustaz was a model father who raised his daughters to make up their own minds and his love for them was unlimited. Madame Atiyatallah would often tell me that it was not he but she who'd brought them up, while he had simply pampered them. In reality, he had raised them with the same qualities as his own. He had brought them up to be modest and kind and to reject ostentation, just as he had instilled in them a sense of pride in themselves. He wouldn't allow anyone to offend their dignity, even himself. Faten remembered well how he'd upset her once in an argument and when she'd come home from work she hadn't gone to greet him in the usual way.

"Hasn't Faten come home yet?" he'd asked.

"Yes, she's back," Hoda had replied, at which he'd gone straight to her room and apologized for what he'd done, saying, "I was wrong, and you were right!"

That's the kind of father Naguib Mahfouz was, nothing like the tyrannical father al-Sayyid Ahmad of whom Madame Atiyatallah said, "That's only in the *Trilogy*."

Twelve

It can't be! What's all this? Who's spreading these stories?

A reporter called me. "Is it true, what we've heard?" he asked.

"What have you heard?"

"Ustaz Naguib . . . has something happened to him?"

"What kind of thing? Nothing's happened."

"You mean, he's okay?"

"Yes, yes, he's fine. But for God's sake, where did you get this from?"

"A reporter friend told me he'd heard it."

"Is this how you get your news?"

"Of course not, that's why I'm checking with you before I write anything."

A few minutes later another colleague called to ask, "What's the latest, Ustaz Salmawy?"

I felt from his voice that he was asking about the same thing, so I said, "The latest is that Ustaz Naguib's condition is stable and the doctors have no cause for alarm."

"There's a daily press conference in the hospital," I added. "Why don't you attend?"

"I went yesterday and heard the same thing that you're telling me now," he said. "But . . . ."

"But what?"

"They say there's a new development."

"Do you imagine the hospital would give daily press conferences about his health and not call an emergency conference if there were any news of this kind?"

None of those who called me were prepared to say what they'd heard. They all tried to suggest it without naming it. But at the same time none of them wanted to miss the news either, so they were trying to preempt it; all of which placed a very severe strain on me.

This wasn't the first time that such unfounded stories had pursued me: before the Ustaz had been moved down to the intensive care unit I'd been surprised once by the newspapers declaring, "Serious deterioration to health of Naguib Mahfouz leads to lapses of consciousness and liver failure." His liver? What was this about his liver? Where had this come from? Then again: "Health of world-renowned novelist Naguib Mafouz takes dangerous turn." What kind of language was that! What was this "dangerous turn" they were talking about?

That day I entered room 612 and found the Ustaz unconscious, the doctors around him. I expressed my anger to them about the articles that the newspapers had attributed to sources in the hospital, and they assured me that they'd kept to their statements precisely and tried to maintain a balance between not causing alarm and the right of the people to know the situation of Egypt's great writer.

But the Ustaz being unconscious every time I came to visit him agitated me more than it should have. Therefore I wasn't able to accept what was said that day.

"What you're publishing isn't accurate," I said. I found myself ignoring everything else in the article and concentrating only on what was said about the liver failure. "Is it true about his liver?" I asked. "This is just groundless speculation!"

Yusif al-Qa'id was there and tried to calm the atmosphere by saying, "Maybe it was just some reporter's error."

"Why do we need to give the man another illness?" I asked. "Hasn't he got enough as it is?"

Such statements had now been regulated by means of the press conferences held in the hospital, but what were these new announcements that were unattributed to any source? All it took was for some "colleague"—as I was told—to say or hear something, to spark a wildfire.

I went in to the Ustaz and found him as I'd left him the day before, asleep. They'd removed the transparent plastic oxygen mask and instead they'd put a large tube about an inch wide in his throat. Was this part of the artificial respiration instrument? Or the device for removing phlegm that he used to resist?

What was the point of this ugly tube blocking his throat, which would completely prevent him from speaking? Even if he were to wake up, he wouldn't be able to speak.

The hair on his chin, which had been shaved about two weeks before, was getting longer. There were still a few hairs that had not yet turned gray and in which I saw a sign that his body was still holding onto life. They say that Marie Antoinette's hair went completely white as she approached the guillotine. But here was the Ustaz, with hair still as black as it had been when he was young, in spite of his medical condition, and in spite of the apparent emaciation of his body.

I cannot carry on watching him like this, as he lies unconscious with this tube inserted into his throat.

I cannot spend any more time in this room.

I cannot stay in the hospital.

I left, but I couldn't go to my office. As I left the hospital I found myself unable to concentrate or even take a decision about what to do now. Where should I go?

My driver saw me come out of the hospital and approached with the car. I asked him to wait till I came back. I crossed the wide street, still not knowing where I was going. It was al-Nil Street and at the same time Gamal Abd al-Nasser Street. Just like so many other things in our country with more than one name and more than one face, and bearing more than one meaning. Why can't we be precise? Why don't we know the truth? Was the Ustaz's condition dangerous or stable? When would he be discharged from the hospital? And I wanted to know, were the doctors saying one thing to us and another to the press? Where was the truth? Was this al-Nil Street or Gamal Abd al-Nasser Street? To some it's al-Nil Street, to others it's Gamal Abd al-Nasser Street. Maybe it was like this with the Ustaz too—for some his situation was dangerous while for others there was no cause for alarm.

There were several riverside cafés on the other side of the street. The weather was hot. I found myself entering one of them. I didn't remember seeing this café before then, but my steps led me toward it and I went in without thinking. I sat at the far end, facing the Nile.

The Nile has an extraordinary ability to absorb all noise. The din of the traffic and the shouts of the passersby died away. I could no longer hear any of it, as if I was in a soundproofed room. For a few minutes I sat without anyone approaching, until I reached a decision that I would opt for the truth that I preferred. This was Gamal Abd al-Nasser Street and the Nile had no need to give its name to any street; and Naguib Mahfouz's condition was stable, not hopeless. That was the truth.

The waiter came over to ask what I wanted. When I didn't reply, he saw that I was distracted and said, "Shall I bring you black coffee without sugar?" By which he meant something appropriate for a solemn occasion.

"Definitely not," I replied. "Bring me something happy."

The man looked at me with surprise.

Fearing he might think me slightly mad, I added, "I mean, juice or a soda drink."

I sat alone, looking at the Nile, and remembered how the Ustaz used to talk about this great river; it was the thing he missed most of all when his eyesight worsened and he could no longer see very far. I remembered how he told me he'd been dazzled by the Nile since he was a child and how he always used to dangle his legs over the railings of the Abu'l Ela Bridge, watching the water flow by, while his mother held him tightly so that he didn't fall in.

His love for the Nile was so great that at the start of his married life he decided to move into a houseboat. He always used to tell me that he'd spent the best years of his life on that houseboat, where he'd lived for seven years, and which faced the houseboats of the prime minister, Ahmad Maher Pasha, and the singer Munira al-Mahdiya. If his wife hadn't decided one day to leave the houseboat, the Ustaz would never have left. But their neighbors' daughter, on the boat next door, had fallen into the river and drowned; he'd returned to his own boat to find his wife holding onto their eldest daughter Umm Kulthum and telling him she would not stay on the boat one day more. Ustaz Naguib was very affected by the death of his neighbors' daughter. In his novel *The Beginning and the End*, the character Nafisa drowns in the Nile. The Nile was the source of life and also its end. In the countryside they appreciated the value of the Nile that brought them prosperity, but at the same time they threw their trash and dead animals into its water. In spite of this the Nile will go on forever . . . life begins and ends while it keeps flowing, on and on.

I was sitting right beside the Nile. I could almost touch the water from where I sat. When the waiter brought my drink I didn't even look at it. I paid my bill and left.

When the Ustaz wakes up on my next visit I'll tell him I've found a place not far from his home where he can be very close to the Nile that he missed so much. I'll tell him that here he can even touch the water.

Thirteen

I was sitting with the family in the waiting room when Dr. Hossam Muwafi entered. After he'd greeted them he took me to one side.

"I need your help," he said.

"What do you mean?" I asked.

"Ustaz Naguib is in a critical phase—he hasn't eaten anything for about ten days now. We're doing what we can with his kidneys but unless his digestive system starts working again, it won't help much."

"How can you expect him to eat when he's completely unconscious?"

"I'm told he woke up yesterday and spoke to them."

"They keep telling me that. But I'm here every day, and on some days I come twice—for several days now I haven't found him awake at all."

"There's a very simple operation that we can do; it doesn't take more than a quarter of an hour."

"What is it?"

"We make a small opening in the stomach and insert a tube to supply his food."

All these tubes in his body, new ones every day!

"Why can't you insert the tube through his nose, in the usual way, instead of doing this surgery?"

"They tried this several times yesterday but it didn't work. Each time they tried it caused bleeding." Then he added, "The operation that I'm suggesting is very simple. My mother had it and she lived for two years afterward."

I hope he doesn't have to be fed through a tube for two years, I said to myself.

The doctor went on: "Without food he gets worse each day. Right now, the only alternative is just to let him drift away while we watch."

The thought of him drifting away as we watched made me angry. "No," I said. "We can't allow that. If there's an alternative, let's do it."

"His wife has refused to authorize the operation," said the doctor. "She says she doesn't want him 'messed up.'"

I went straight back to the waiting room and tried to persuade Madame Atiyatallah of the need for the operation, on the basis that it was the only choice we had. If his condition wouldn't improve with the operation, it certainly wouldn't improve without it. Hoda and Faten joined me in trying to persuade her, until finally she agreed. Within minutes the surgeon had been called and the operating theater, on the same floor, had been prepared.

Everything was ready and I was on my way out of the room to have a look at the theater that the Ustaz would be moved to. There, in front of the room where the Ustaz was lying, I found television cameras ranged like machine guns, facing the door that he would soon emerge from on the trolley.

I exploded with anger. What was this? Who gave permission? I asked the photographers to leave immediately and went to the hospital manager who was standing by the theater with the other doctors, supervising the preparations. I asked him who had authorized the TV crews to bring their cameras here, right to the door of the Ustaz's room, while he was in this condition.

I told him that unless the whole area was evacuated the Ustaz could not leave his room. The manager himself was very upset by the sight of cameras pointed at the intensive care unit in this way, and in a few minutes the whole of the second floor had been emptied of the press, while a guard had been placed to block access to the operating theater.

Hoda had told me a short while before how, only the previous day, a young woman had penetrated the security around the intensive care unit with the excuse that her mother was inside, before it was discovered that she was hiding a camera inside her handbag in order to photograph the Ustaz.

When the Ustaz finally entered the operating theater, the doctors invited me to wait in their room. We drank tea together and when the operation was over I was introduced to the surgeon, who I was able to thank. I then accompanied the Ustaz as he was wheeled out, back to his room.

As soon as the Ustaz was back in his bed, Dr. Muwafi went to check on him. He lifted the sheet from the Ustaz's body and examined the tube in his stomach. It was no more than a centimeter wide and ended in three openings. As I watched, the doctor fitted two of them with capsules to block them up. He left the middle opening free, which would be used to supply the food by means of a syringe.

"We need to wait twenty-four hours before injecting any food, to give the wound time to heal," said the doctor.

"He has diabetes," I said, "so maybe it'll take longer."

"I usually prefer thirty-six hours," he said.

"What are you going to feed him?"

"In the beginning, yogurt mixed with honey, then afterward anything, as long as it's mashed up well."

"He didn't use to eat anything sweet at all."

"The body breaks honey down quickly and it doesn't leave a trace." Then he reassured me by saying, "A nutritionist will prescribe the meals to be injected every two hours."

I was going to comment that the Ustaz used to eat very little and I was afraid that if his food was forcibly injected every two hours it might overload his digestive system, especially since he'd been rejecting food for almost ten days now. But the doctor added that the nutritionist would take into account that he hadn't eaten anything for some time.

Instead I said, "When do you think we'll see a result from the feeding?"

"In just a few days."

So, just a few days and he would improve after beginning to eat again. This would mean he'd regain consciousness and, who knows, maybe it would be just a few days more until he was able to leave the hospital in the same condition that he'd entered it. He wasn't suffering from a chronic or incurable disease. He'd entered the hospital to have "a couple of stitches" at the back of his head, and his current condition bore no relation at all to what he'd gone in for. It was just a few minor complications—the bronchitis was not a long-term problem, his kidneys would revert to normal after he started eating, he'd regain consciousness and thank the doctors one by one as he'd done before, and then he'd return home.

And on the Saturday immediately following his discharge I'd ring his bell at exactly six o'clock, his wife would open the door and I'd go into his reception room at the same time as he entered it from his office, tying the cord of his silk dressing gown around his waist. Then he'd kiss me on both shoulders as usual and sit on the right of the sofa, with me on the left, on his hearing side. I'd tell him the world's news that he never liked to be without. And he'd forget, as I would too, all the trials that had afflicted his spirit and his body. With a contented smile on his face he'd relate to me again that Dream, which I had recorded in his own voice and which hadn't appeared in *Dreams in the Time of Convalescence* because I still had it with me:

> I saw myself in a hospital, undergoing some tests, and there I learned that our national leader Mustafa al-Nahhas was lying in the next ward, so I went to him. I was moved by how he looked and said, "Get well soon, Pasha!"
>
> "What I'm suffering from," he said, "is the inevitable fruit of ingratitude."
>
> "God never leaves a good deed unrewarded," I said.

Fourteen

The American publisher Sidney Schiff called me, in a hurt and angry tone.

"How did you let Naguib Mahfouz get into this state?" he asked. Schiff had learned from some newspapers in the United States that the great novelist's condition had worsened since he'd entered the hospital and that he was now in a complete coma, unaware of anything around him.

"It's not as serious as that," I said. "He's not in a coma; it's just that he's not always conscious. That's all."

"Why doesn't he come to the United States?" he asked. "Naguib Mahfouz is a human treasure and here we have the best that medicine can provide."

"It had been suggested that he should go abroad but the doctors thought he wasn't suffering from anything that couldn't be treated in Egypt."

"Then why don't you cure him if the cure's available there? Why is he getting worse?" Then he added, "I'm speaking on behalf of a lot of publishers who are genuinely worried. . . . You'll have to wait decades to see another Mahfouz in the Arab world."

I began to feel annoyed at his tone, which was reproachful, so I said, "Pray with us that he'll recover from his illness."

"He needs more than prayers," he said, appearing to reflect my annoyance. "And we hold you responsible!"

What was this responsibility that Schiff talked of? The Ustaz would get better, all being well, after the operation, especially now that he was taking food again. He had an iron will—I'll never forget how, after the attempted assassination, this elderly man, who was already over eighty and who'd won the highest accolade in the world for his writing, learnt how to write all over again with his injured hand, never once complaining or grumbling.

The incident had partially disabled his right arm, preventing him from writing for some time. But he'd submitted himself to daily physiotherapy sessions, and the doctors had advised him to exercise his hand by writing, saying that this would help him to recover its use. Every time I visited him I saw his little notebook, in which he would practise by writing the names of some of his friends or their phone numbers.

One time, when he'd already been doing these exercises for a few months, I found him with his face radiant, saying, "Come and see, I want to show you something!" Then he'd pulled out the ruled notebook, in which he did his daily exercises, and said, "Do you notice anything new? I'm staying on the line!"

I almost shed a tear but managed to control myself as I expressed my happiness to him at this great achievement. Being unable to write could have destroyed him forever, but his uncomplaining determination enabled him to recover the ability. I was now hoping that he would recover his health through the same force of will. It was true that he was now ninety-five years old but his mother had lived till she was over a hundred, while two of his brothers were almost ninety.

When he'd reached ninety I'd asked him on his birthday, "What do you feel, now you're ninety?"

"I feel like I'm at Sidi Gaber. When I used to go to Alexandria every year I would always get off at the last stop, Mahattat Misr. When the train reached Sidi Gaber, the last station but one, I knew there was only one more station before I had to get off, and that I had just enough time to get my things together."

Naguib Mahfouz at Sidi Gaber was the title I chose for his collection of literary musings, which I used to publish in English in *Al-Ahram*

Weekly newspaper and which the AUC Press published in 2001 on the occasion of his ninetieth birthday.

Five years had gone by since then, since he'd reached Sidi Gaber station, but who knows whether the train was now approaching the terminus? In my view, it was not. This was not yet the last station.

This is what I reflected on, as I went back to the hospital. How I wished I would find him awake and be able to talk with him. He'd ask me what was going on in the world and what the foreign papers were saying, whether in the field of culture and literature, of politics, or of new inventions, which he was especially interested in—for he always believed in scientific progress.

Sometimes I'd read to him from works of foreign literature that had caught my eye and that I thought he might like. What he often asked me to re-read for him was my English translation of the late nineteenth-century Cuban revolutionary poet José Martí, who wrote:

I grow a white rose
In July as in January
For the sincere friend
Who gives me his honest hand.

And for the cruel one, who tears out
The heart with which I live,
I grow no thorns or nettles.
I grow a white rose.

I told him that I'd look for an Arabic translation of the poem but he liked to hear it in its English translation. Every time I read it to him I felt that Martí could only have written this poem about Naguib Mahfouz, who'd filled our lives with flowers to cheer us up. Even for the cruellest of his critics, his only response was a bouquet of white roses.

I had taken with me again *Dreams in the Time of Convalescence.* Perhaps he'd ask me to describe what the book looked like and maybe I'd talk to him about it a little.

I reached the hospital to find the news that he'd suffered a hemorrhage in the colon and that throughout the night the doctors had tried to stop the bleeding by inserting an endoscope into his intestines to cauterize the source of the bleeding.

O God! When would these ignominies come to an end? Should I tell the doctors to stop violating his body and just leave him to die? Forgive us, you who caused no harm to anyone in your entire life. Forgive us if we harm you or cause you pain.

I could not enter the room. I could not face him. How could I explain what had happened? But who said I needed to explain it or justify it? He, more than anyone, understood human weakness and would sometimes find excuses for it. He would say of those in the field of literature who criticized him after winning the Nobel prize: "We need to understand their position. They're only human and maybe some of them had been promised the prize before me."

Today, Ustaz, I ask you to forgive us as you forgave your critics. It is only human frailty and you know we can't help it. We want to keep you with us—life without you will be deprived of the fluttering flag that has raised our name up high in the world, just as it will be deprived of he who planted the white rose for us.

I looked in from the doorway of the room. He was asleep, receiving blood to compensate for what he'd lost. The room was quiet and the blood was passing drop by drop into the needle in his right hand.

I advanced with a heavy step till I reached the side of his bed. His face seemed pale but I recognised that sincere smile that I'd seen when he forgave his critics after the Nobel prize.

The doctor told me that the Ustaz was still under the effect of the sedative he'd been given after the operation. That damned drug, which I care nothing for. I bent toward his left ear and said, "Good morning, Ustaz Naguib."

"He can't hear you," said the doctor. "He's still unconscious."

"I know," I replied. "What I don't know is why he had the hemorrhage."

"Maybe it was an old ulcer in the colon. It took us a while to discover that the hemorrhage was in the colon. We were very surprised by a rectal hemorrhage that we couldn't see a reason for."

Another doctor said the reason for the hemorrhage was the large amount of antibiotics he'd been given and the length of time he'd been on the respirator.

I was still wondering about the hemorrhage when the doctors went out. Was it his body's way of rejecting the food that we'd forced into his stomach? Was it the body's revolt against what had happened against his will? Naguib Mahfouz was not a big eater at all and never ate between meals. In recent years he only used to eat a few morsels, so were we wrong to insert that tube into his stomach and feed him every two hours? And what could we do now? Should I rid him of this tube in his stomach?

How I wished he would speak and ask us to do something for him. Had he spoken and we hadn't heard him, or hadn't understood? He'd spoken when he shouted out so politely, "I beg you, leave me alone. . . . That's enough!" Or maybe he'd spoken through gestures when he kept taking off the oxygen mask, and when he'd said he wanted to "go." Now, when we'd silenced him with the sedative and tied his hands to the frame of the bed, he could communicate only with his blood. Were we listening? Could we understand?

Fifteen

Madame Atiyatallah told me that the last time she'd heard him speak before he lost consciousness was when he'd called out to people long passed away; she'd recognized the poet Salah Jahin among them. When the nurses had heard him calling out they'd tried to speak to him but he hadn't responded and just kept talking to those departed souls. Now he was no longer speaking, either to me or to those who'd departed. In his mind, was he with them, or maybe it was the coma that the foreign papers had written about? Although he was unconscious I felt he was still with us and aware of my presence whenever I entered the room. He didn't need to speak or greet me in any way in order to make me feel that he knew I was there, or that he was aware of everything around him.

In his ear I told him what he had so often asked about: "Ustaz Naguib, the fighting in Lebanon will end today. They've agreed to a ceasefire."

Only a few years ago, the international Spanish director, Pedro Almodóvar, made a film entitled *Talk to Her*. The film is based on the medical theory that someone in a coma has lost the power to interact with their surroundings in the same way as a paralyzed person who cannot move, but knows exactly what is happening around them. By ignoring them we simply confirm their isolation from their surroundings.

Instead, by continuing to address them, we keep them in contact with life and encourage their recovery.

In Almodóvar's film a male nurse is in love with a young ballet dancer who has entered a coma and is being cared for in the hospital. Each day he comes to visit her and tells her stories about what he's seen, such as how he went to the ballet, as if she can hear him. The film ends with the dancer coming out of her coma.

I wonder, can I wake the Ustaz up by talking to him? He used to love hearing stories, which had compensated him for being deprived of reading because of his deteriorating eyesight. I saw tears in his eyes on only two occasions: the first was when he described the death of his favorite national hero, Saad Zaghloul, while the second was when I told him the story of my play *The Chain*, which was performed in 1996, in which the young hero dies at the end in the midst of gunfire between the police and the al-Gama'a al-Islamiya, while his mother screams like a wounded animal: "My country!"

I was taken aback when, at the end, I found his eyes brimming with tears as he said, "Forgive me, it's a very moving ending."

That's right, I'll talk to him as if we were sitting in his home. I'll talk in the usual way, as if he was conscious. For years I'd been talking to him about everything he wasn't able to read or watch, so why should I stop now?

I bent down to his left ear and said loudly, "The Arabic edition of the Dreams has been published, Ustaz Naguib, and here's the first copy off the press."

I placed the book in front of his eyes, but he didn't open them. I imagined that he asked me about how it looked as he always did whenever I brought him a new book, so I started to describe its appearance and its size. Then I opened it and turned the pages:

> I saw myself in the Abbasiya district, wandering in the open spaces of my memory, recalling in particular the late departed 'A.' I called her on the phone and invited her to meet me by the fountain, where I welcomed her longingly and suggested that we spend the evening at Fishawi's café, as we had done in the old days. . . .

Before I could finish the Dream I thought I saw him smile. "By the way," I said, "you didn't tell me who 'A' was. It's true that I didn't ask you; there are lots of things that I haven't asked you about." Then, to myself I added, "How strange life is! It never allows us time to do what we want."

"I should've asked you what 'A's' full name was—I really wanted to know more about her since you'd written so much without mentioning her name. I noticed that she was married to someone else in Dream 191, and I'm sure she's the subject of Dream 144:

> Peering into the shadowy past, I saw my sweetheart's luminous face, though she'd been dead for fifty years. I asked her about the letter I'd sent her a week ago.

I imagine too that she's in Dream 14:

> I was walking along the green banks of the Nile. The night was damp as the secret dialogue continued between the moon and the river's waters, on which the luminous rays rippled. My spirit wandered through the recesses of Abbasiya, suffused with the scent of love and jasmine.
>
> I found myself debating the question that had assailed me from time to time—why hadn't she visited me in a dream even once since she died, at the very least to confirm that she was real, and not merely an adolescent fantasy?

I didn't read the rest of the dream. It has a sad ending, when his loved one finally appears in the middle of a raucous procession. He approaches her and puts his arms around her:

> . . . then heard the crackle of something breaking. Her dress felt as though it was draped over empty space—and no sooner had I discovered this, than the marvellous head fell to the ground and rolled into the river. The waves bore it away like a Rose of the Nile—leaving me to eternal grief.

Because of the atmosphere of sadness I didn't dare talk to him about this surreal ending—in spite of its artistic beauty. I preferred to keep the talk on a lighter, playful level between two friends. "So, who's 'A' then?" I asked. "Is it Aida Shaddad, the lover of Kamal Abd al-Gawad, which is you in the *Trilogy*? Or is she someone else entirely, like Abla for example? Or maybe another less well known name, like Anbar or Anad?"

Then I said, "Imagine, Ustaz Naguib, that Hagg Sabri, who you dictated this dream to, thought that 'A' was her actual name, not just an initial, and so he wrote it with an 'a' followed by a 'y,' therefore 'Ay,' and this is how it was published!"

I imagined that he smiled, so I asked: "Why are you smiling? Were you having a joke with this initial, when her name was actually Ay, as Hagg Sabri wrote without realizing that he'd stumbled on the secret?"

The doctors came in suddenly and our conversation was cut short. He didn't have a chance to reply. Maybe if they hadn't come in he would have laughed one of his ringing laughs that I hadn't heard for more than two weeks now. When the nurses entered just before the doctors, one of them had heard me talking to him. She asked in disbelief, "Is he awake?"

"Do you imagine I was talking to myself?" I asked.

I left them in the room. One of the guards told me, "We haven't heard his voice for a few days. What's the matter, Ustaz Mohamed?"

"A temporary problem," I replied.

I sat alone in the waiting room and when the doctors emerged I asked them, "How is he today?"

"There's some improvement," they said.

Sixteen

On my way to the hospital I asked myself, "What will today bring? Will I find any improvement?"

Improvement in my view was not a matter of his blood sugar going down or his temperature returning to normal, or even that the bleeding had stopped or they'd taken him off the respirator. For me, improvement was a matter of a single factor: that he was conscious again and able to talk to us, just as we talked to him. It would mean he'd decided to come back to us from where he'd been for the past ten days. If he came back his temperature would go down by itself, the bleeding would stop, and he'd breathe normally, not through some machine.

It was Gandhi who said, "Each night, when I go to sleep, I die. And the next morning, when I wake up, I am reborn." What I was waiting for now was to find him reborn from this long sleep. I wanted him to be conscious again. He might wake up without being conscious, be able to see us and speak to us, without recognizing us. I knew this was not what he wanted. He told me once that on his last visit to Tawfiq al-Hakim in the hospital, al-Hakim had asked him when he walked in, "Who are you?"

Mahfouz had commented to me, "God keep us from this!" Maybe therefore we should thank God that he'd kept his memory up until the moment he'd entered this sleep, which had gone on so much longer than we'd expected for reasons we couldn't understand or do anything about.

All we can do is pose the questions without providing any answers. We can only ask what the guard had asked me the day before: "What's the matter, Ustaz Mohamed?" Yes, what *is* the matter? Who can tell us? Maybe only he, the father of stories, the greatest storyteller, as the French writer Robert Solé had called him; and this is the greatest story, for which we don't know the ending. It's up to you, great storyteller, to provide the ending as you've always done, in your stories about the magnificent districts of old Cairo where the whole of humanity can discover the noblest principles and the greatest ideas. Over thirty novels, more than 350 short stories and five plays, each one a fabric interwoven with events, and you always provided the ending. This is the great tapestry . . . but where's the ending? Have you already provided it without us knowing?

I hurried into the room and for the first time I didn't greet the guards standing at the door, as if I was afraid to miss a word that he might utter or a movement he might make.

I found him just as I'd left him the day before. I don't think he'd even changed position in bed. He was still asleep on his back, with the great tube in his mouth, smaller tubes in the veins of his neck and other tubes in his hand, and the pipe hanging from his stomach. The only noise in the room was the faint rhythmic sound of the machine above his bed. His face was even paler and the artificial respirator was pressing on the right-hand side of his mouth.

Even so, I greeted him: "Good morning, Ustaz Naguib!" I didn't feel he was aware of me in the same way I'd felt before. I couldn't bring myself to talk to him this time, when he wasn't really present in the room. This was his body, or what was left of it, after he'd suffered for a month and a half—forty-five days exactly, during which time he'd lost weight and a lot of his color, as well as his vitality and consciousness. He'd entered the hospital on 16 July and it was now 29 August; and he'd left us for somewhere where we couldn't communicate, whether in words, movements, or sensations. Today I was possessed by a terrible feeling that we would not communicate again, that he had departed.

His birth had been difficult on that day, 11 December 1911. A leading doctor, Dr. Naguib Mahfouz Pasha, was called to carry out the delivery, at a time when the custom was that a midwife would come to the house. His birth took a long time and when it was over the parents decided to name the child after the great Coptic doctor, out of gratitude.

O God, do not let him depart this world in the same distress that he entered it. Let him go peacefully as he wished, without any pain.

I sat beside his bed and looked at the copy of the Dreams that I'd left there the day before, hoping that he'd wake up and ask for it just as he'd asked for his glasses and hearing aid. But there it was, exactly where I'd left it. I flicked through it, and saw Dream 70:

> The longing to see my dear ones called to me, and I set off in the direction of the ancient quarter. As usual, I took a short cut on foot until the old house appeared, along with my memories.
>
> I wasted no time in starting to climb toward the third and final floor. But halfway up the stairs, I was stricken by an exhaustion that would not pass, and which made me think about putting off the journey. If it weren't for my stubborn character—which hates to go back on a commitment—as well as for the intensity of my effort, I would not have made it until I reached the third-floor landing.
>
> From my new vantage point, I could see the apartment door immersed in quiet and calm, and I realized that there were only ten more steps before the end of the staircase. Yet I did not see a single stair, finding in their place a deep pit. My heart pounded with fear for the people of the house.
>
> Though it was now impossible to reach my goal, I did not look behind me. I did not think of going back, nor did I lose hope. I kept my eyes fixed on the door drowning in silence and tranquillity—as I cried out, and cried out, and cried out again from somewhere deep within me.

Some nurses entered. I didn't know what they were doing. I was waiting for him to call out, hoping I'd hear him. I saw for the first time that they didn't speak to him as they usually did, even that simple baby talk that Hoda disliked so much. Did they have the same impression as me, that he was no longer with us? Was this the end? No . . . surely the end could not be like this.

My God! With Your great mercy and Your extraordinary power, let him stay among us, since we have no other like him. You gave him ninety-five years . . . but we need more. We cannot replace him. Leave him with us for another year or two, so that we can celebrate him throughout the world. Leave him with us for a few months until he reaches his ninety-fifth birthday. Give us the chance to make him happy as we say to him, "May you live for a hundred years!" Leave him with us for a month, so that we can strive to do for him what other nations of the world do for their great men and women, and which *we* don't do until they've already gone!

Seventeen

That same evening I received a call from one of his guards at the hospital who said, "My condolences."

I dropped the phone, then picked it up again. "I'm on my way!" I said. "Please don't," said the man. "Wait. They'll inform you officially."

"I'm not waiting," I said.

"Please wait," he said, "or I'll be in trouble. You'll soon be informed officially."

It was around ten in the evening and I knew there was no one with him in the hospital. His wife had gone home at about eight thirty. After that, the room—as I later learned—had witnessed some unusual commotion, with an emergency situation. Several doctors had rushed in with equipment. Some of them left while others arrived, and this went on for half an hour before things calmed down. No one was allowed into the room and when the end of the shift came and the new guards arrived the old shift was not allowed to leave the hospital.

I asked the guard, "Have his family been informed?"

"They'll be informed officially."

I put the receiver down, bound by the promise I'd made not to take any action that would show I'd been informed.

This waiting was the longest I'd known during the whole time the Ustaz had been in the hospital.

A whole hour passed without me receiving the official notification. I thought about calling the Ustaz's house, but it was late and I couldn't bring myself to disturb the family with news that I wasn't even sure of myself, despite my confidence in the person who'd informed me.

I called the hospital but for the first time I didn't find a single doctor to speak to. None of them were at their desks. Where had they all gone? Were they still in his room? Or were they avoiding me?

I remembered a dream that hadn't been published in either the Arabic or the English editions of the Dreams. It may have been the last dream that he'd dictated—he'd given it to me a week before the accident. I'd read it once when he'd given it to me. I'd then put it away and not looked at it again. Now it began to urge itself on me, so I read it as I sat by the phone:

> I saw myself walking in the street just before dawn. My ears caught the sound of a beautiful voice singing "Visit me at least once a year." I turned around and saw a person wrapped in a sheet that covered him from head to toe, so I looked at him with great interest. He uncovered his torso, revealing no more than a skeleton. I jumped back in fear and spun round, pursued by the beautiful song, "Visit me at least once a year."

I would go to the hospital and what would be would be. I could not leave him to spend the night alone there. Maybe he was still alive or still in the final stages. For a person to find himself alone at the time of his departure must be a terrible thing. But my going there would certainly raise suspicion—in the hospital they're not used to me visiting in the middle of the night. This could cause trouble for the person who, thankfully, had told me the news.

I couldn't sleep that night. Each time I dozed off I imagined that the Ustaz was free of his illness and returned to full health, moving and speaking to us as he used to . . . then I would wake up to the nightmare, before dozing off again to a reality that was much more pleasant, as I confused doubt and certainty, wakefulness and sleep, fact and fantasy, in a daze that lasted throughout the night.

Eighteen

At nine o'clock the next morning my mobile phone rang. It was Dr. Zakariya Azmi, the president's *chef de cabinet.*

"My condolences," he said. I thanked him without further comment.

"He'll have a military funeral. We want to arrange it for tomorrow after the midday prayer, at al-Rashdan Mosque in Madinat Nasr. What do you think?"

"I'll talk to the family and get back to you," I said.

I couldn't tell whether Dr. Azmi was wondering about my response, which hadn't shown a trace of surprise at receiving such news. Maybe he suspected that the news had already been leaked to me. Suddenly he asked, "When did he pass away?"

Without thinking I replied, "Yesterday evening."

"What time was it?"

"Before ten."

He didn't comment.

When the call had ended I rang Madame Atiyatallah immediately. She was still at home. I asked her how she was, trying to find out whether she'd been informed yet. She replied that everything was fine. I realized that she did not yet know.

"I'm on my way to the hospital," I said.

"Is anything wrong?" she asked.

"They told me the Ustaz wasn't doing too well."

He'd had a crisis at around seven o'clock the evening before. His family was with him in the room. The doctors had asked the family to wait in the waiting room, while several of them gathered round the Ustaz. After a while they told them that everything was fine, so the Madame and the daughters went in to check on him. Hoda and Faten had then left the hospital, followed by the Madame at around eight thirty.

Maybe Madame Atiyatallah had thought when I said he "wasn't doing too well" that he'd had another crisis like the one the previous evening.

"When are you going to the hospital?" I asked.

"I was just getting ready to go now," she replied.

"Let's meet there then," I suggested.

The news is now confirmed and it's I who must inform the family. Is this what I was waiting for last night while I couldn't sleep, while the official notification was on its way? So the Ustaz has passed away and I won't see him again. I won't hear his welcoming voice when I visit him in his home and he won't kiss me on the shoulders anymore.

A few days before, Faten had told me in the hospital that on the Saturday before he'd lost consciousness he'd told the doctors he was waiting for a guest to arrive, but they hadn't really understood what he'd meant. When Faten had arrived at the hospital they'd asked her who used to come to visit him on Saturdays.

He won't ask about me again, nor wait for me on Saturdays. Never again will I hear his voice or his ringing laugh.

He's gone to be with those who loved him and whom he missed so much, those whom he used to call out to, maybe to tell them to wait for him. His journey is now over, as in Dream 110:

> At the end of an exhausting errand, I came to a locked gate. Gathering all my remaining strength, I shook it till it began to open.
>
> Beyond it I could see a lake, from which missiles were being launched into space. As each one exploded in the air,

it lit up the face of a former lover—the heavens were filled with those I adored.

Yet still I wait for the glowing face of the one who taught me love, who made me long to live forever.

I arrived at the hospital and headed straight for his room. A sheet covered the whole bed but it looked empty. Where had they taken him? I lifted the sheet and there he was. His face had a look of tranquillity. He didn't appear to have suffered any pain, but he'd lost all his color. His mouth was open as it had been the whole of the final week due to the thick tube connected to the respirator. Why hadn't they closed his mouth when they removed that damned tube?

His face was calm, expressionless, just like when he'd said he wanted to "go," before he left . . . when he lost consciousness and left.

The features of his face were blurred as they appeared to me through the tears that filled my eyes.

There is a poem, "The Golden Legend" by the American poet Henry Wadsworth Longfellow, that says:

. . . time has laid his hand
Upon my heart, gently, not smiting it,
But as a harper lays his open palm
Upon his harp, to deaden its vibrations.

So the harp of the great Arab novelist has fallen silent and no one will hear it again.

But when did it fall silent? Was it today or when its owner asked to "go," some two weeks ago?

Throughout that time we'd resisted his wish to leave. When he stopped eating we put a pipe in his stomach and forced him to take food. When his stomach rejected the food and his colon had a hemorrhage, we put an endoscope inside his body and cauterized the bleeding. When he stopped breathing we supplied air to his lungs through an artificial respirator. When his heart stopped beating we administered an electric shock to restore the heartbeat.

Did we make the right decisions? We used every treatment available in order to resist fate—was it the right thing to do, morally? In former times, did death not simply take our forefathers and they died in peace?

What have all our medical advances achieved, when we simply delay the painful moment of death by a few days, maybe months or years, so that the body goes on living even after the soul is happy to accept its end? The moment of death is one of awe. Perhaps we should simply face it with humility.

Buddhist monks in Tibet have traditional rituals that help the dying to depart, so that he does not resist the moment and prolong his agony.

Faten came in, so I covered his face quickly and wiped away the tears that had fallen from my eyes.

"I want to see him," she said.

"There's no need," I responded. "Hold on to the smiling face that you know and remember. This face is the face of death, not his face."

Then Hoda arrived, carrying a copy of the Quran. She sat quietly on the chair beside the bed and started to read in silence. Faten joined her.

Madame Atiyatallah told me that she too had noticed when she entered the room that the bed seemed empty, and had imagined that they'd moved him. Does the soul give the body its form and the space that it occupies, leaving the body like a deflated balloon when it departs? What is the body other than a cloak for the soul, which, when it departs, leaves it flat on the bed where it lies? I tried to look away from his body, but I couldn't. I looked at Hoda and Faten, then back at him.

This emaciated body in front of me, from which the soul of Naguib Mahfouz has departed, is bereft of its solidity, size, and mass; it has become flattened like a bed and will not rise again.

Nineteen

"When did the Ustaz pass away?" I asked the doctors.

"This morning," they replied.

"So what happened yesterday evening?"

"His heart stopped beating, but we managed to revive it."

"What time was that?"

"About seven in the evening, while his family were in the hospital."

"But I'm asking about what happened during the night."

"It was critical—we did all we could."

One of them added, "We took him off the respirator and waited. If he'd managed to last for six hours without needing it, it would mean he wouldn't need it again, but he got worse. . . . "

"When exactly did he pass away?"

"Just after eight this morning," they replied. "About ten past, when his heart stopped again, but the equipment wasn't able to revive him this time."

I said nothing.

The doctors went on: "We need to move him to the cold chamber."

It seems that coping with death lasts only for a moment. We look at the deceased and then the administrative procedures take over, as we transfer our concern from this solemn moment to the funeral arrangements—

the burial, the announcement in the newspapers, the condolences—in a breathless rush that finishes only after several days when the ceremonies are over and the relatives of the deceased find themselves for the first time in front of the abiding and inescapable fact that their loved one has died and that they will not meet him again for the rest of their lives.

I went to tell Madame Atiyatallah and her daughters that the president's office had informed me there would be a military funeral at the Armed Forces Mosque in Madinat Nasr. "But he wanted people to pray over his body in al-Hussein Mosque," his wife said.

Without hesitation I assured her, "So, we'll pray in al-Hussein first."

I called Dr. Zakariya Azmi and told him that we would pray over Mahfouz's body first in al-Hussein Mosque according to his wishes, before going to the Armed Forces Mosque for the military funeral.

We went to the large waiting room on the first floor of the hospital building. General Mu'tasim Abd al-Muti arrived, the assistant for medical affairs to the minister of the interior. With him were the hospital manager and a group of doctors. They proposed special arrangements for the funeral and the burial. The waiting room seemed like the control room for the process, and just a few minutes later all the Ustaz's friends were present: Gamal al-Ghitani, Tawfiq Salih and his wife, who never left the side of Madame Atiyatallah from that moment to the end of the burial ceremony the next day. There was also Yusif al-Qa'id, the publisher Ibrahim al-Mu'allim, and Amr Tawfiq Abd al-Aziz, the Ustaz's nephew.

I discussed with the police officers the arrangements for the military funeral in the morning and the preparations for moving the body from the hospital to the old quarter where the late novelist had been born, and where prayers would be said over the body in al-Hussein Mosque, before going on to al-Rashdan Mosque in Madinet Nasr in good time before the midday prayers.

Then I went with General Abd al-Muti to his office in the hospital where he made all the necessary calls to implement the plan. The secretary of the minister of culture called me to tell me of the minister's decision that the ministry would cover the costs of all the funeral arrangements. I replied that I would convey this to the Ustaz's family but that the funeral was going to be a military one and that the president's office would cover the costs, while the Writers Union would take care of the mourners' tents.

The day was half over. Dr. Hossam Muwafi came to say that it was time for the press conference. He asked me to accompany him to the conference hall to announce the news to the media.

The hall was bustling with journalists, television cameras, and foreign correspondents. Dr. Muwafi had requested from me a few days before that I ascend the podium with him, to give reassurances about the condition of the Ustaz. Now I was standing to announce his death.

"On behalf of the Egyptian Writers Union," I said, "I announce to the Egyptian people, the Arab nation, and all of mankind, the death of the honorary president of our Union, one of our national icons, who lifted the name of our country up high like a flag among the nations of the world.

"Our great novelist Naguib Mahfouz has passed away after an illness that lasted a month and a half, as he approached his ninety-fifth year.

"Prayers over his venerable body will take place tomorrow at al-Hussein Mosque, as he wished, from where he'll move in a military funeral from al-Rashdan Mosque in Madinat Nasr, wrapped in the flag of Egypt, on a gun carriage pulled by horses and preceded by a military band.

"This will conclude an extraordinary chapter in the history of Arabic literature after almost a century of a gift that has enriched our lives and filled them with joy. We will always owe him a debt of gratitude that we can never repay."

The questions began, starting with the following:

"What time did he pass away?"

"Dr. Hossam Muwafi will be responsible for answering all your medical questions concerning the time and cause of death." I stepped down quickly from the podium.

When I got back to the room his body had been removed. The room was empty.

Twenty

That afternoon a senior officer from the explosives unit in the presidential guard called. He asked me to meet him at the hospital in the evening in order to conclude the arrangements for taking custody of the body until the end of the funeral the next afternoon. I wondered how our great novelist had not enjoyed such concern for his safety while he was alive, especially before October 1994 when a young man had been able to approach him with a knife in the street and, in front of passersby, stab him treacherously in his neck, leaving him unable to write.

I thanked the officer and told him that in the evening I would be at the Ustaz's home beside the hospital and that I'd be able to meet him around eight o'clock in the hospital manager's office.

The reason for my visit to the Ustaz's home that evening was to help his family select the medals that the Ustaz had won, which would be delivered to a representative of the military ceremony, so that they could be carried with the coffin as is traditional in military funerals. Since the Ustaz had won a large number of medals and prizes, the family and I needed to select the most important ones—a difficult task because some of them had been lost over the years, including the golden Nobel medal, for example, that bore the face of Alfred Nobel. The funeral of our Nobel prize-winning writer would take place without his Nobel medal. But we did manage to find the Nile Necklace, which was the basis for the military funeral, although it was missing the medal that was supposed to hang from it. The other medals that were delivered for the ceremony included that of the *Commandeur des arts et des lettres*, bestowed by the former president of France, François Mitterand, and many other medals and prizes from other countries, such as the Cavafy Prize from Greece and the Latin American Literature medal, as well as Egyptian medals such as the Mubarak Prize, the State Appreciation Prize, and the Order of Merit.

I'd been happy when the representative called me to ask for these medals before the funeral—at the time of Tawfiq al-Hakim's death in 1987 we'd been surprised by the organizers of the funeral asking about the medals when we were already in the Omar Makram Mosque, just before the funeral cortege was due to depart. The members of al-Hakim's family had said the medals were at home and that no one had told them to bring them. The funeral of Tawfiq al-Hakim had therefore left without the medals that are traditionally carried by officers on velvet cushions.

We did not know how the Ustaz's medals had disappeared. No one had ever entered his home before he won the Nobel prize—some of his friends didn't even know where he lived, but immediately after the award was announccd his homc bccamc a public place in the eyes of some, open to anyone who wanted to visit him, even without his permission or invitation. I remember the day the award was announced the Ustaz was about to go to his weekly meeting with the Harafish group at Qasr al-Nil café. Since he didn't like to change his routine for any reason as soon as it was six o'clock he left home to go the café. His family had not got used to not answering the door to anyone who called. Some visitors, both Egyptian and Arab, came to have their photographs taken with the Ustaz; his wife would always open the door to them, ask them in and offer them something to drink until the Ustaz came in on his way out of the apartment, whereupon they would take their photographs or ask him for his signature or to autograph a book.

This is what happened on the day the Nobel prize was announced, but in an unprecedented way: the apartment filled with dozens of people that no one knew, including ordinary members of the public as well as journalists and photographers. Madame Atiyatallah remembers that one of the photographers climbed on top of the bookcase to photograph the crowd that filled the apartment. After a while it became difficult even to shut the front door—the crowd extended from the bedrooms inside as far as the street in front of the building, while the Ustaz was still at his meeting with the Harafish in the café, receiving an equivalent number of people.

That day, neither Hoda nor Faten were at home. Hoda learned about the prize while she was at work. She tried to call home to congratulate her father but couldn't get through. Faten, on the other hand, had no idea. When she arrived home from work and saw such a huge crowd she was very alarmed—she thought perhaps the gas canister in the kitchen had exploded and caused a terrible accident.

Many documents disappeared from the apartment that day, including important ones like the Ustaz's marriage certificate and the Madame's birth certificate.

These incidents occurred on many occasions, such as the Ustaz's birthday or his two previous discharges from the hospital. Things disappeared from the house each time. Sometimes his family would be surprised to find a photo of the missing document in the newspapers. This was one of the reasons why Madame Atiyatallah preferred the Ustaz to stay in the hospital while he was recovering from the operation. She knew she could not handle his visitors at home.

For a long time that evening we stood in front of a medal that we couldn't identify, until we remembered that it was the Spanish Arts and Literature award given to him in 2001 by the former prime minister, José María Aznar.

In the spring of that year the Spanish ambassador had called me to say that his government had decided to award Naguib Mahfouz with its highest award for arts and literature. In normal circumstances the ambassador would have bestowed it himself but the prime minister had expressed his desire to postpone the ceremony until his official visit to Egypt that summer. He wanted to bestow the medal himself.

I remembered Aznar's visit to the Ustaz's home. His wife Ana Botella de Aznar was with him. They stayed for almost three quarters of an hour, telling Mahfouz how much they admired his work and how they'd read everything that had been translated into Spanish.

Hoda, Faten, and I finished choosing the medals that would be delivered to the representative. We'd selected eleven. I then excused myself to attend my meeting in the hospital, with the representative of the presidential security guard.

Twenty-One

The man was well mannered and had a colleague with him, although he was the only one who spoke. He told me that he didn't want to receive the body without me being present. I asked him what he meant by "receiving" the body.

"We'll secure it and provide a guard while the body is in the cold chamber until the morning when it will be carried to the funeral. During that time he will be our responsibility—no one will be permitted to approach the body."

He added apologetically, "These are unavoidable security measures."

"But the rituals prior to the funeral," I said, "like the washing, the shroud, the hearse, require people to be with the body."

"We'll provide complete security," he said, "until we deliver the body after the funeral."

"What will happen after that, until it reaches the tomb?" I asked.

"Our task ends with the conclusion of the military funeral and the departure of the president," he replied.

This was the first time it had been mentioned from a credible source that the president would attend the funeral.

At that point the hospital manager interrupted to say that the hospital was prepared to supervise the transfer of the body to the tomb.

The representative of the presidential security then asked me, "Who'll be present at the washing?"

I replied immediately, "Me."

The man began to choose his words carefully as he apologized once again: "You know of course that work is work. There are security measures that need to be taken wherever the president goes."

"That goes without saying. There's no need to apologize."

The man immediately went on: "Since you'll be with the body during the washing, which will be after we've secured it, our procedures might require us to subject you to a search."

"It's routine, nothing more," he added.

"We're all used to being searched," I said. "We have to remove our shoes and some clothing in various airports around the world. As for the body, since it's currently in the care of the hospital, the task of delivering and receiving it is between you both. I'm willing to be present if you wish. All I ask is that we revere the sanctity of death while carrying out these procedures and give the respect due to the body of the deceased."

"Don't worry," said the representative.

The conversation ended at that point. A few moments went by in silence, broken by the representative saying, "There's no need for us to keep you any longer."

"Didn't you ask me to be present at the delivery of the body?"

"All we'll do is place our guards at the door of the cold chamber."

"Is that all?" I asked.

"That's all," said the man, echoed by his colleague who hadn't said a word throughout the meeting.

A few more moments of silence passed before the man added, "That's all that concerns you. The rest, as you said, is between us and the hospital."

I excused myself and went out into the street, where I was hit by a blast of hot August evening air.

Twenty-Two

I reached the hospital at around eight thirty in the morning to make sure we'd taken all necessary measures to get us to al-Hussein and then to the Armed Forces Mosque in Madinat Nasr before midday prayers.

The Ustaz's family were already there. Madame Atiyatallah thanked me—the hospital had told her that I would attend the washing ceremony myself. Tawfiq Salih and his family were there too. "I'll come with you," he offered.

I took him to one side and warned him, "We may be searched before we go in." He looked surprised. "Don't be alarmed," I added. "As far as I understand, it's only security procedures that have to be followed. If you're coming with me, we should get going or we'll be late."

We went down to the ground floor with the hospital team and from there to a courtyard at the back that had been spread with rugs. The walls of the building that overlooked the area had been covered with tent cloth. We had arrived at the door of the cold chamber. I found some of the Ustaz's friends there, including the writer Zaki Salem, who used to meet the Ustaz every Monday evening. "I couldn't see him for the whole time he was in the hospital," he complained, "since visitors were banned. I came more than once but they wouldn't let me in. All I want now is to say a final goodbye."

"I understand how you feel, Ustaz Zaki," I said. "But unfortunately it won't be possible now for anyone to see him or get near him."

At the door of the chamber was a car that had been equipped to carry the wooden coffin that was now on the ground, with ten athletic-looking young men standing around it. They were the members of the guard responsible for the coffin until it was delivered to the military ceremony in the Armed Forces Mosque before the funeral. They were all wearing dark grey suits and not in uniform. They all seemed to be clones of each other, tall and broad-shouldered.

A man came out of the cold chamber. He was in his sixties, in a white *gallabiya* and a little overweight. If you'd seen him in the street you'd have taken him for a butcher! I looked at him expectantly and he said, "I wash the body."

I turned to Ustaz Tawfiq Salih who apologized: "I can't go in. But my son Muhammad will go with you."

"There's no need," I said. "As long as I'm there."

But Ustaz Tawfiq insisted: "No, no. He wants to come with you."

Muhammad Tawfiq Salih expressed his sincere wish to be beside me during the washing. I looked at the man who was responsible for the washing and suggested, "Let's get started, so we won't be late."

I waited for someone to search me, as I'd been warned the day before, but no one did; so the man opened the door and we went into the cold chamber.

The room was cold but not freezing, its walls covered in white tiles like a bathhouse, and on two sides were metal drawers the length of a human body. The man took off his *gallabiya* and opened the lower drawer on the left, asking me and Muhammad to help him move the body, shrouded in its white cloth, from the drawer to a table where he would perform the washing. I saw the face of the Ustaz as I'd seen him the day before, on his bed in the intensive care room. The man turned on the tap of a wash basin in a corner of the room, to his left, brought out a loofah that he was careful to show us was new, and started the washing.

I think the man was reciting the Quran or some prayers throughout the procedure, but I'm not sure. Maybe he wasn't saying anything at all. I don't remember. I was so preoccupied by the awesome sight in front of my eyes that my ears were deaf and my other senses failed me.

From time to time the man said, "Help me lift."

Each time I touched his body I wanted to shout, "He's still alive, his body is as soft as ours!" But when I looked at his face, or what had been his face, I realized he'd gone and left us his outer form, and I remained silent.

His body was white and pure like that of a saint. It was surely of him that Spain's leading Renaissance poet, Luis de Góngora, wrote, "*Un cuerpo con poca sangre / Pero con dos corazones*" ('A body with little blood / But with two hearts'). But his right hand was noticeably swollen, bruised, and blood-colored. This hand that had raised our profile on the world's literary scene, and that some of the greatest writers of the world had kissed before my own eyes! Why did it now seem twisted as if disabled, its color so different from the body in front of me? How many decades would it be until we saw another hand like his? The American publisher had been right and the minister of health wrong, when he'd said there was no need to go abroad for treatment and that the Ustaz wasn't suffering from anything we couldn't cure at home. He was suffering from old age, in which illnesses affect the body differently from the young; this is why there is a specialization in medicine called geriatrics, since among the elderly there are complications that don't affect the young and therefore require different treatment. This specialization is not found in our faculties of medicine.

I asked Dr. Hossam Muwafi once, "Why don't we have doctors or hospitals that specialize in treating the elderly?"

"Because we don't have any elderly," he replied. "Here, people do not age as they do abroad."

So the Ustaz's problem was that he had grown old in a country that didn't know how to deal with old age.

We hadn't dealt with him any better when he was well than when he was ill—we'd accused him of being an unbeliever and a heretic, and condemned him to death without trial.

While the man continued to wash the body, I imagined the Ustaz's voice, which I hadn't heard now for more than two weeks, coming back to me; I could hear him as clearly as I had heard him when we were recording one of his Dreams (number 88):

> In our village, every individual was waiting for the letter that would settle their personal destiny. One day, I received my own letter—and read it to find I had been condemned to death by hanging.
>
> Word spread far and wide, as was customary among us. The members of our village club met and decided to celebrate the event when it happened.
>
> In my house, where I lived with my mother, brothers, and sisters, breasts were gladdened and all were pleased. On the much anticipated day, the drums pounded in the club. I came out of my house wearing my finest clothes, surrounded by the members of my family.
>
> But then my mother, separating herself from our state of mind, began to cry. If only my father had lived long enough, she wailed, to see for himself this glorious day.

When the washing was over, the man fetched some clean water and removed all traces of soap before sprinkling rose water on the body. He asked us to bring the shroud that was behind us. Muhammad went to get it. The man commented, as if he was promoting his goods, "This is some of the best cloth. The deceased was a great man." He then wrapped the body in the cloth a few times and tied it firmly over the head and feet, before putting his *gallabiya* on again.

The door of the cold chamber opened, like a pharaonic tomb that had remained closed for thousands of years, and we went out into the open air.

Twenty-Three

What worried me as we were preparing to leave in the car that carried his coffin from the hospital were the crowded streets between the city center, al-Azhar Street and al-Hussein Mosque, and the crowds that would be gathered at the mosque, especially after the press had announced wrongly that morning that a "popular funeral" would be held in al-Hussein Mosque before the military funeral. Would we be able to get through the crowds, which would be bound to swell due to the numbers coming to the funeral?

The body was placed in the coffin and it was closed firmly; a green velvet cloth was spread over the top, embroidered with verses from the Quran and prayers. The guardsmen moved it to the car and we started off at exactly nine thirty in the morning for the old quarter where Naguib Mahfouz Abd al-Aziz Ibrahim al-Basha was born almost ninety-five years ago, where he'd spent the best years of his life and to where he kept returning even when he'd left the area. And here he was now, after departing this life, determined to return once more to the same place.

We all set off behind the hearse, which was preceded and followed by security cars. There were some ten cars in all. Despite my preoccupations I made out a few faces, some of them friends and relatives: counselor Hussein Abd al-Aziz, the eldest of the deceased's nephews and joint inheritor of the estate along with Madame Atiyatallah, Umm Kulthum, and Fatma; Amr and Ali Tawfiq Abd al-Aziz, the grandsons of Mahfouz's oldest brother; his closest friends, Tawfiq Salih, Gamal al-Ghitani, Yusif al-Qa'id, and Zaki Salem; and other family members of the deceased and some of their wives.

It took less than a quarter of an hour to reach al-Hussein. The streets had been completely emptied of traffic—all cars had been stopped on one side and all traffic lights set to green. Al-Hussein Mosque had also been emptied, while a great cordon had been placed around the area in front to prevent anyone from reaching the mosque.

We all got out in front of the mosque and the doors of the funeral car were opened. The guardsmen who'd placed the coffin in the car at the hospital now took it out.

The coffin, shrouded in green cloth, had just appeared when dozens of members of the public rushed through the security cordon and into the mosque before the guards could stop them. As the coffin was taken into the mosque it was surrounded by no less than a hundred people, like messengers from the rest of the crowd who remained behind the cordon, unable to reach the body.

Inside the mosque, the guards placed the coffin by the pulpit. A few moments later Sayed Tantawi, sheikh of al-Azhar, entered with the mufti, Dr. Ali Gom'a, and the minister of *awqaf*, Dr. Mahmud Zaqzuq. They all said a few words about Mahfouz: the sheikh of al-Azhar offered a eulogy for the great novelist and prayed to God to "join him with the prophets and believers in paradise." The mufti also praised the late novelist's achievements in the service of his country, while the minister of *awqaf* stated that the country considered him to be the fourth pyramid, for his everlasting and unforgettable contribution to modern Egyptian civilization.

The sheikh then led prayers for the soul of the departed. When he'd finished, Gamal al-Ghitani was beside me. "Let's carry the Ustaz out of the mosque on our own shoulders," I suggested. "When we reach the military ceremony, no one will be able to get near him." He agreed without hesitating.

I went to the head of the guards and asked, "Will you allow the Ustaz to be carried out of the mosque on the shoulders of the writers of Egypt?"

"Wait a moment and I'll let you know," he replied.

He soon returned. "Unfortunately, it won't be possible," he said.

The guards had started to pick up the coffin so I left the man and went with Gamal al-Ghitani. We lifted the coffin together with the members of the guard and carried it out to the courtyard in front of the mosque. The area was now filled with dozens of others who had succeeded, during the prayers over the body, in getting to the entrance of the mosque. On the other side of the cordon were hundreds, or maybe thousands, of people who'd failed to reach the body.

From afar I saw some people carrying banners that they intended to display during the popular funeral that the morning papers had written about. The banners proclaimed the spontaneous words of ordinary people, who may have known Naguib Mahfouz or met him in this part of the city: "Mahfouz is always in our hearts . . . beloved son of Egypt!" "To eternal heaven, son of our alley!" "Farewell, O Shakespeare of the Arabs!"

I then noticed the young writer Ahmad Said who'd often attended the Ustaz's meetings on Sunday evenings at the Shepheard Hotel. He had fixed a huge portrait of Mahfouz to his chest and was trying to break through the barriers. In tears, he embraced me. By the next morning this picture of Ahmad Said with Naguib Mahfouz's picture on his chest had been published in many Arab and foreign newspapers.

After no more than half an hour, which we had spent in the mosque, the coffin returned to the car again. Finally we all set off for the Armed Forces Mosque in Madinat Nasr, along streets emptied of cars and pedestrians, arriving at the mosque in no more than a quarter of an hour.

Twenty-Four

The security arrangements were very precise and orderly but this tight control meant that we reached al-Rashdan Armed Forces Mosque—which I'd feared we would reach late because of the crowds—three hours before the time of the funeral. It was not yet ten thirty and the funeral would set off after the midday prayer; that is, at around one thirty.

When we reached the mosque there were no more than thirty or forty left from those who'd accompanied the body at the prayers in al-Hussein. The car carrying the body entered the mosque compound from the entrance that had been arranged for the funeral, in front of which were barricades to prevent other cars gaining access. The guards directed us to a side street where there was another entrance to the mosque. There too, there were guards preventing cars from getting through, so we got out and entered the mosque compound on foot.

The family of the deceased were sitting in one of the halls of the mosque, while all the men were gathered in another hall. We must have waited more than an hour before the mourners arrived, one by one. Most of them were officials, led by the prime minister and other ministers, as well as ambassadors and people from the world of arts and culture. There were no more than fifty altogether.

I was standing with Yusif al-Qa'id when some representatives of the presidential office asked us which family members the president should offer his condolences to after the funeral. Yusif al-Qa'id responded: "The nearest relative is counselor Hussein Abd al-Aziz." He escorted them to him. Madame Atiyatallah had given me the names of the Ustaz's nephews—Amr and Ali—so I added those two names as she had indicated.

It was hot and we had to sit in the sun outside the mosque, receiving the mourners who arrived every few minutes. From time to time I went inside to sit with some of them.

An ambassador from a major western country asked me, "Why is it a military funeral? Was Mahfouz an officer originally?"

"In Egypt, a military funeral is the highest funerary honor," I replied. "Among those that it is given for are the winners of the greatest state award—the Collar of the Nile—which President Mubarak bestowed on Mahfouz after he won the Nobel prize in 1988."

After almost three hours it was time for the midday prayer, so the mourners began to ask, "Where's the body? When will the funeral prayer be held?" At the same time, those who had performed the prayer with us at al-Hussein Mosque were also starting to wonder if a funeral prayer could be performed twice. One of the security officials said that it was and that the sheikh of al-Azhar had just gone to lead it, so everyone hurried into the mosque to pray. One of them asked me, "Aren't you coming with us?"

"I've already prayed the funeral prayer in al-Hussein Mosque, as he wished," I replied.

When they emerged from the prayer a short while later, we were asked to go to the street where the hearse had entered and from where the funeral itself would start. We all started to move toward where they had directed us. As we walked, the prime minister, Dr. Ahmad Nazif who was leading the group and who was beside me, remarked, "Today I feel Egypt has lost one of its most valuable deposits."

"But today our deposit has matured," I retorted. "Its value has continued to increase with time and we have reaped the benefits year after year for almost a century. After today Naguib Mahfouz will be transformed from a great writer into one of the literary legends of the world, like Dante, Shakespeare, or Goethe, with added value for Egypt. The important thing is to know how to reinvest it."

When we arrived at the place where the coffin was, the green covering had been removed and replaced by the tricolored flag of Egypt. The coffin was now lying on a bronze gun carriage, with two soldiers bearing the medals that we'd delivered the day before. Behind the carriage stood the mourners, with the officials and some members of the armed forces and police at the front, all waiting for the president to arrive. The prime minister was shown to his place while I stood with the rest of the mourners, lined up behind the officials as if we were in a military parade awaiting orders.

The sun grew hotter and the metal of the gun carriage glared more brightly. Gamal al-Ghitani was standing beside me. We stared at the coffin lying on the carriage in front of us and at the horses ready to pull it, and noticed the pharaonic decorations.

"This is how the funeral of Ramses II must have been," said Gamal. "When Egypt wants to honor one of its sons officially, they treat him like a pharaoh!"

A few minutes later a group of black cars passed quietly beside the rows of mourners. As the cars reached the front, where the body lay, the president got out of the first car, while his son Gamal Mubarak appeared from the second. The president took his place among the mourners, in the front row between the minister of defense, Field Marshall Hussein Tantawi, on his left, and prime minister Dr. Ahmad Nazif on his right, while in the row behind them stood Gamal Mubarak. The president then put his right foot forward and, as the military band played the funeral march, the procession started to move and the funeral began.

After a few minutes, when we'd advanced about fifty meters, the procession came to a halt, while the head of security led the deceased's nephews to a small shaded podium, where the president offered them his formal condolences. The president then got into the black car that had been quietly following alongside, and departed, while the rest of the mourners stayed to greet, in turn, the relatives of the deceased on the podium.

With the departure of the president and the disappearance of the guards, the orderliness was thrown into disarray, the coffin vanished, and we had no idea where the gun carriage or the officials had gone. We found ourselves stranded among the journalists and television cameras that the security had kept out until the president had left, and who were now suddenly allowed to enter, bursting in like a raging torrent! We all searched for each other and for our cars. No one knew how to get to the grave—we had planned to walk behind the funeral car. The appearance of order that the presidential security service had provided had now completely vanished and I had to excuse myself from doing an interview with the press in order to look for the car that was going to carry the body to the grave, somewhere on the Fayoum road.

The old cemetery for the Ustaz's family had been in the Mugawirin district, but the area had been developed and the graves relocated. Tawfiq Salih had then suggested that the Ustaz should buy a plot next to his own grave on the Fayoum road.

Among the chaos all I could see were other people searching for the same thing as me. Finally I spotted my driver in the distance. He'd returned to look for me after having been held back with the other cars. With him was the driver of Ibrahim al-Mu'allim, who asked me where his boss was. I also asked the drivers if they'd seen any of the people who'd been with us. My driver told me that Ustaz Tawfiq Salih had gone in the hearse, which had just left. When I spotted Ibrahim al-Mu'allim giving an interview to a satellite channel, I indicated to him that his car had turned up. He cut the interview short and came over. I got into his car with him and told my driver to follow us. The driver rescued me by giving me my mobile that had been left in the car according to the security instructions.

Now that I'd got my phone back, I started calling everyone on the way to the cemetery to find out where they were and to ask where the cemetery itself was. When I called Tawfiq Salih, his wife answered, saying that her husband had left the phone with her. She reassured me that Madame Atiyatallah was with her and that Hoda and Faten were following in another car. I asked her for the location of the grave, since it was beside the plot that her husband had taken. After she'd given me directions she asked me where her husband was. I replied that he'd been seen getting into the hearse. Ibrahim al-Mu'allim then called Yusif al-Qa'id and found him on the road to the cemetery with Gamal al-Ghitani. In this way, on the desert road to Fayoum, we gradually reassembled the pieces of the puzzle that the gusts of summer winds had scattered in all directions.

Twenty-Five

We arrived at the tomb in advance of the body. The only people there were security guards and some of the Ustaz's close friends including Gamal al-Ghitani, Yusif al-Qa'id, and Aziza al-Yassergi, who used to attend the Wednesday evening meetings at the Sofitel in Maadi. That was how Naguib Mahfouz's friends referred to one another, as the "Wednesday people" or the "Friday people," according to the day they used to meet him. If you knew to which day someone belonged you'd also know whether they were one of the writers who met on the Farah Boat on Tuesday evenings or one of the Harafish who met on Thursdays at the home of Tawfiq Salih.

The tomb was surrounded on all sides by desert. What had made Tawfiq Salih choose such a remote area, thirty kilometers outside the city? Egyptians have always lived among cemeteries and buried their dead beside the living, so that death would not separate them. On festivals and holy days they continue to visit their parents and relatives, as if they're still alive. The cemeteries of Cairo, in Imam al-Shaf'i, Basatin, and other parts of the city, are at the same time residential areas. Is it the pharaonic idea of death as merely a transition, after which one returns to life, just as night divides one day from another?

The tomb was modest, befitting the modesty of its owner, and built of red brick. Above it was a sign that announced plainly and simply: "The tomb of Naguib Mahfouz." The word "tomb" took me aback. I'd never imagined associating Naguib Mahfouz with such a word—a man who'd loved life so much, with all its ups and downs, as he used to say. But who said that death is the end of the matter? That was not something he believed in. In the epic *Harafish* he'd written, "Death doesn't conclude life, or else it would conclude itself."

Above his name the sign displayed verses from the Quran (55:26–27): *Everyone upon it will perish / And there will remain the face of your Lord, Owner of Majesty and Honor.* To the right was written the word "Allah" while on the left was "Muhammad."

A tent had been erected beside the entrance to the tomb, to protect visitors from the burning summer sun. There were a few chairs inside.

I left the tomb and the marquee behind me, and went out into the desert.

> Death. What a frightening truth! Never before had I felt its terror. What is this mysterious riddle? What is it exactly? What is the nature of the spirit that will leave us all after a while, to return to its Creator?

Naguib Mahfouz wrote these words in an early story called "The Wisdom of Death." It must have been one of his first published stories. It appeared in 1938 in a magazine called *al-Riwaya*, but was subsequently forgotten and left out of later collections, until the Ustaz's nephew Mahmud al-Kurdi sent it to me.

In the story the narrator—who is close to death—concludes by asking himself, "What have I done with my life?' He continues: "Some people might ask this question and find a satisfying answer in the innovative ideas that they have bequeathed to mankind, or the glorious works that they have performed for their countries, or their noble struggles for their families and children."

When he wrote this story, which he called "An Egyptian Tale," at the age of only twenty-seven, was the Ustaz aware that he was writing about himself and the ideas he had "bequeathed to mankind"? Who knows? In any case, his life had now come full circle. We had never imagined he would leave us. He had reached his final station, while we had thought the train would never leave Sidi Gaber. He had known that however long the train was delayed at Sidi Gaber, his was the next and final station—the train would terminate and he would take his leave.

But he had achieved so much before leaving the train, had bequeathed so many innovative ideas. Amongst all our writers he was unique in having lived through all the major historical events of our age, for almost a century: the resistance to colonialism at the start of the twentieth century, the 1919 revolution, the period between the two world wars, the 1952 revolution and the social and political changes that followed, the October War, the Open Door policy and Camp David, up to the present day. If you wanted to look back over this period you could find it in his more than thirty novels: in the *Trilogy*, *Modern Cairo*, *Miramar*, and *The Day the Leader Was Killed*; in his short stories that numbered more than 350, such as "Love Above the Pyramid Plateau" and "The People at the Top" and in his neglected plays, which were some of the most beautiful one-act Arabic plays.

So many foreign ambassadors, including the former French ambassador Bruno de Leusse, had told me that they came to understand Egypt by reading Naguib Mahfouz's work. De Leusse remarked that in the works of Naguib Mahfouz he'd found what he hadn't found in books of history or politics, namely humanity. It gave him a real understanding of Egyptian history because it is people who make history, with their dreams, their ambitions, and their fragility.

But the value of Naguib Mahfouz lies not in the social documentaries of his literary oeuvre but in what he contributed to Arabic literature itself, by opening up new avenues for the novel that had previously been unexplored. Mahfouz's works included the historical, the realistic, the experimental, the philosophical, and the epic, as well as other works that transcended traditional genres observed by more ordinary writers. For geniuses rise above established rules and create new rules, which then become established for those that follow.

That was the nature of Naguib Mahfouz, and always will be. We need only to look at the condition of the Arabic novel before and after him to realize the unquestionably enormous effect he had on Arabic writing. This giant of a man, to whom destiny had granted every reason to be proud, was the most modest of God's creations. I still remember his first comment upon winning the Nobel prize: "My masters deserved this more than me," by which he meant al-Aqqad, al-Mazini, Taha Hussein, and Tawfiq al-Hakim.

At a time when we used to value our writers by the degree to which they followed in the footsteps of the west, by how far they resembled Tolstoy, Dickens, or Flaubert, Naguib Mahfouz succeeded in forging a characteristically Arabic novel among the novels of the world, leading the American scholar Roger Allen to comment that "Mahfouz succeeded in creating what we can call the Arabic novel."

For most of the twentieth century, Naguib Mahfouz inspired successive generations throughout the Arab world and contributed to their emotional development. His influence also extended far beyond the 300 million citizens of the Arab nation and penetrated the emotions of the outside world that he had never even visited.

With his departure we have reached a turning point in our literary history. The last of the literary greats of this wretched age has gone. He has gone, the son of Gamaliya and al-Hussein, who introduced the world to the residents of its backstreets and alleys. He has gone to meet those whom he had venerated and whose contributions he had respected. He is now with al-Manfaluti, Taha Hussein, al-Aqqad, al-Mazini, and Tawfiq al-Hakim; with al-Bohtori, Abu Nawwas, al-Mutanabbi, and Bashar Ibn Burd; while we remain, recording in our sorrowful ledgers the loss of another icon of our bereft nation.

By means of his stories this great novelist had managed to embody an ancient Arab heritage, from the *Thousand and One Nights* to the *Conversation of Eisa Ibn Hisham* and the *Hilaliya* epic, adding to the literary heritage of the world that he was so inspired by, and creating for us in the end a modern literary form that helped give the Arab novel a unique character identified by critics the world over.

He also embodied ancient Egyptian culture, whose monuments he had loved since the time he used to visit them as a young boy with his mother, recreating some of the most beautiful moments of its rich history in his early works.

The words of his Nobel address, which I was to deliver at the venerable Swedish Academy in Stockholm, still ring in my ears as he spoke to the world: "I am the son of two civilizations: the Arab Islamic and the ancient Egyptian!"

From these two civilizations he created something contemporary and magnificent that we can be proud of before the world, raising our status among its nations and enhancing the prestige of our culture. He became what only a few have become, a symbol of the nation itself. No one will talk of Egypt and Arabic literature without mentioning the name of Naguib Mahfouz.

And now he is wordless, as silent as the sands around the tomb where he lies, out in the desert. The source has dried up, arid and unable to bear more fruit. He who gave words their most wonderful meanings and revealed the loftiest ideas has departed; he who gave life to inert letters, making them pronounce their love for this land and its inhabitants, and for its ancient backstreets and narrow alleys.

Today, how can we use those same words and letters with which he formed those noble works so venerated by the world? Who among us would dare to call himself a writer of the same mold as our late great writer? Who could give voice to those words that our extraordinary master brought to life out of his love for the good people of his country?

The Arabic novel is now enshrouded in a coffin, while we await its arrival at the graveside. Arabic literature will never be the same again.

Twenty-Six

After a long wait the car arrived, bearing the coffin, and I made my way back to the tent. It was not the same car that had carried him from the hospital to the funeral. There were no guards now, nor cloned young men. Tawfiq Salih was sitting in front beside the driver. We lifted the coffin down from the car. The flag of Egypt had been removed after the military funeral and he was now wrapped again in the green cloth. Now we could approach as we wished and touch it with our hands.

We placed the coffin inside the tent and waited for his family to arrive, in order to begin the burial rites. Aziza al-Yassergi ran her hand along the coffin as if sending a greeting to its occupant, while groups of people whom we did not know gathered around the tomb. They might have been relatives. More and more arrived. I asked Madame Atiyatallah who they all were. She said she didn't know. One of them was weeping loudly, so I asked him if he was a friend of the Ustaz.

Through his tears he replied, "I wish I'd been his friend, as you all were. Unfortunately I met him only once, many years ago, at Qasr al-Nil café. But I knew him as well as you did. I read everything he wrote and I felt closer to him than to many people I know in person."

"How did you know where to come, when even some of his friends didn't know?"

"I know everything about Amm Naguib, God have mercy on him. I was always wanting to correct the newspapers whenever people got something wrong about him."

After a short while the car carrying Hoda and Faten arrived and we were about to start the burial when some of the Ustaz's oldest friends called, saying they were on their way and begging us to wait for them. When they turned up a few minutes later they said they'd wanted to attend the funeral but had been prevented by the security guards, and that there were many others who'd failed too.

We lifted the coffin onto our shoulders and were moving toward the tomb, when gunshots rang out in the desert silence. Beside the tomb stood a guard of honor, who had been appointed to fire a volley of shots at the moment of the burial. This was part of the military funeral. At the sound of the shots, the body was lowered into the tomb.

Suddenly a group of photographers leapt onto the entrance of the tomb to photograph the body as it was being placed in the grave. I asked them to get down immediately, pointing out that no photography was allowed inside the tomb and that they should have some respect for the departed. They did as I asked, without complaining. Some of them left while others switched off their cameras and stayed, in order to attend the burial.

The coffin had been opened and the body removed, and there was the shroud in which I had seen him wrapped from head to foot.

Hoda and Faten were sitting on chairs inside the tomb, each of them with an open copy of the Quran, from which they read verses until the body had been buried and the grave had been sealed. Madame Atiyatallah remained outside, incapable of entering the tomb. As soon as the body had been lowered into the grave, Gamal al-Ghitani broke down. I put my arms around him and led him to a seat away from the grave. At that moment Gamal, as he later wrote, saw the many years he'd spent with Mahfouz descending into the grave with his body.

None of us dared to enter the grave with the body, apart from one middle-aged man whom I saw humbly remove his shoes in order to descend. When he emerged I thanked him warmly and he told me his name. He was a doctor who, like countless others, had admired the Ustaz without ever knowing him. I embraced him and we said goodbye, expressing a hope to see each other again.

The grave was then closed over the great man. It was sealed over the body in order to release the soul from the shackles of time and place, and to set it free for eternity; but for those who loved him and for his friends, he had gone forever.

Everyone shook hands, some of them overcome, others in tears. They started departing from this desert on the Fayoum road, each to return to his place in the tumult of the city.

"Can I give you a lift?" Ibrahim al-Mu'allim asked.

"No thanks," I replied, "I'll go in my own car."

There was less activity around the tomb now and the guards who'd helped people to find it had left, along with those who'd fired the volley of shots during the burial.

I sat on a chair in front of the tomb and looked at the façade that had just been closed over the Ustaz, whom we would never see again, unless, perhaps, in our dreams.

For the past few years Naguib Mahfouz had lived with his Dreams. Would he now return to us through our own, his face radiant with that smile of love and hope, or had this face vanished forever? Would we meet again, after death and in spite of it? Or was this the final parting?

On my way home I played a cassette of him reading some of his Dreams, which I'd kept in the car. He was reciting the first of the dreams that he'd had to memorize in order to dictate it to Hagg Sabri, when he'd lost the use of his hand—that hand that had continued to write until time removed its strength and its words were no more. Once again I saw his face, in spite of death, and heard his words:

> I saw myself in the Abbasiya district, wandering in the open spaces of my memory, recalling in particular the late departed 'A.' I called her on the phone and invited her to meet me by the fountain, where I welcomed her longingly and suggested that we spend the evening at Fishawi's café,

as we had done in the old days. But when we reached the familiar place, the deceased blind bookseller came over to us and greeted us warmly—though he scolded the dearly departed 'A' for her long absence.

She told him that what had kept her away was Death. But he rejected that excuse—for Death, he said, can never come between loved ones.

I rewound the tape a little and once again he spoke: "Death . . . can never come between loved ones."